CHANGE YOUR CAREER

BABY BOOMERS!

HELLO BABY BOOMERS!

This is your first positive step to CAREER CHANGE SUCCESS

Allow yourself to be motivated and inspired. Prepare to move forward and take the steps to a new and rewarding career. Focus on the tools, techniques and strategies provided. Utilize the Five Step Approach to guide you on your journey and achieve your goals.

Written by
John Rodsett

Published by Blue Mountain Media, Publishing Division

Corporate address:
11520 Jefferson Blvd., Suite 224,
Culver City, CA 90234

Copyright@2014, Film Biz Seminar Inc. All rights reserved

No part of this publication may be reproduced, stored in a retrieval system, or transmitted in any form or by any means, electronic, mechanical, photocopying, recording, or otherwise, without the prior written permission of the publisher.

Library of Congress Cataloging-in-publication
John Rodsett
CHANGE YOUR CAREER...Baby Boomers!/John Rodsett

ISBN-13: 978-1494780234
ISBN-10: 1494780232

For information on all Film Biz Seminar Inc. publications, seminars, webinars, educational activities visit www.johnrodsett.com

Printed in the United States of America

CAREER CHANGE

THINGS YOU NEED TO KNOW & QUESTIONS THAT NEED ANSWERS

WHAT IS THE MOST IMPORTANT QUESTION

WHY DO YOU NEED THIS BOOK

WHO IS JOHN RODSETT

WHAT IS THE FIVE STEP APPROACH

WHAT IS YOUR DREAM CAREER

HOW DO YOU OVERCOME OBSTACLES

WHAT SKILLS, TALENTS, EXPERIENCE DO YOU NEED

HOW TO GET ON THE FAST TRACK TO CAREER CHANGE

WHAT IS THE GOLDEN OPPORTUNITY FOR BABY BOOMERS

WHAT ARE YOUR CAREER STRENGTHS AND WEAKNESSES

HOW DO YOU IDENTIFY YOUR CAREER GOALS

WHAT IS THE NEW CAREER WORLD ORDER

WHAT TYPE OF PERSON ARE YOU

WHAT ARE YOU DOING AFTER FIFTY

IDENTIFY YOUR CAREER ROADMAP

WHAT IS THE BLUEPRINT FOR CAREER CHANGE SUCCESS

CONTENTS

INTRODUCTION — 19
- BABY BOOMERS — 19
- ONCE A UPON A TIME — 21
- WHO IS JR — 23
- WHY DID I WRITE THIS BOOK — 24
- WHY THIS BOOK IS DIFFERENT — 25
- WHAT IS THE MOST IMPORTANT QUESTION — 26

WHY NOT YOU — 29

BEING A BABY BOOMER — 41
- WHO ARE BABY BOOMERS — 41
- WAKE UP CALL — 41
- CAREER OPTIONS — 42
- GOLDEN OPPORTUNITY — 44

MY CAREERS — 47

THE NEW WORLD CAREER ORDER — 51

FIVE STEP APPROACH TO SUCCESS — 55

STEP 1: WHAT DO YOU WANT — 57
- WHAT IS THE MOST IMPORTANT QUESTION — 57
- EXAMINE YOUR CAREER — 59
- WHY A CAREER CHANGE — 63
- YOU ARE UNIQUE — 63
- DECISIONS — 66
- FIND THE INDUSTRY, THEN THE JOB — 67
- BE HAPPY — 68
- SELF EMPLOYED OR EMPLOYEE — 69
- LEFT SIDE RIGHT SIDE — 71

STEP 2: WHERE ARE YOU NOW — 73
- EVALUATE YOUR SITUATION — 73
- RE-INVENT YOURSELF — 74
- CAREER MYTHS — 78
- WHAT KIND OF PERSON ARE YOU — 79
- WHAT IS SUCCESS — 80

MY CAREER AFTER FIFTY — 81

STEP 3: WHAT YOU NEED TO HAVE — 87
- DO YOU HAVE WHAT IT TAKES — 87
- ACTIVITY v's ACCOMPLISHMENT — 91
- WHAT DOES EDUCATION MEAN — 93
- YOU NEED CAREER MANAGEMENT — 95
- YOU NEED TIME MANAGEMENT — 98
- WORK HARD / WORK SMART — 99
- DO YOU NEED TO BE PERFECT — 100
- WE ALL HAVE TRANSFERABLE SKILLS — 101

STEP 4: HOW TO GET THERE — 105
- WHAT IS A CAREER ROADMAP — 105
- WHAT ELSE IS REQUIRED AS PART OF YOUR ROADMAP — 107
- WHAT DOES A CAREER ROADMAP LOOK LIKE — 108

STEP 5: WHAT YOU NEED TO DO — 111
- PERSONAL CAREER BRAND — 111
- CAREER OPPORTUNISM — 115
- THINK — 118
- MAKE YOUR OWN LUCK — 118
- HANDLE STRESS — 120
- LEARN FROM MISTAKES — 122
- WORK TO LIVE OR LIVE TO WORK — 123

SUMMARY — 127

JOHN RODSETT – RESUME – BIO — 133

WHY READ THIS BOOK

Good question!
Certainly if you are reading my book, I would assume you have an interest in a career change.

> Not sure how to move forward?
> Confused as to a potential strategy?
> Looking for guidance?

I've been there and done that!

If you are contemplating or in the process of deciding to change careers then this book is for you. This book is a first class ticket to career change success.

> Ten years ago I had no career and no place to live
> Sounds pretty dramatic... and it was!

For over twenty years, I lived in Los Angeles and had a great career in the media industry. Then one day, just over ten years ago, something happened! I realized my career was coming to an end due to technology and demand changes - plus I was totally burnt out with living in Los Angeles!

> Does any of this sound vaguely familiar?
> Are you contemplating a major change in your career?
> Do you have feelings of concern and apprehension about where your career is heading?

I had many such thoughts - all at the age of fifty.

In the last ten years, I have had to face the realities of being a baby boomer moving into my fifties and having the world around me change significantly. I felt there were so few options that it created a paralysis of fear and an inability to act, even though I felt something needed to be done.

Does that sound familiar?

Three important events have happened in the last decade that made me re-focus on my career and in so doing inspired me to write this book.

Firstly, significant technology changes plus demand decline in video and DVD sales, forced me to totally re-evaluate my career. This happened by 2003.

Secondly, globalization fundamentally changed industry and competition effecting business and the employment environment in the USA.

Thirdly, the financial meltdown of 2007 onwards caused major disruption to industry and created serious negative effects to the employment marketplace and to the "American dream" ideal.

I guarantee that this book will help provide a structure, a guide, to the process and the journey of changing careers. It will identify tools, techniques and strategies that will provide a framework for your successful transformation from one career to another. The Five Step Approach helped me and I know it will help you.

For boomers, the time to act is now. Golden opportunities await the maturing boomer in terms of new employment avenues and personal growth. Opportunities, especially as entrepreneurs and being self-employed, are continuing to open up like never before. Take today's circumstances and make them yours – be positive and move forward with career change.

FEATURES OF THE BOOK:

- ✓ How to approach and execute career change
- ✓ What is the most important question?
- ✓ Find out what golden opportunities lay before you
- ✓ What major changes have happened and how can you benefit?

- ✓ Follow the Five Step Approach to success:
    - What do you want
    - Where are you now
    - What you need to have
    - How to get there
    - What you need to do
- ✓ How to create and execute a career roadmap
- ✓ Identify your dreams and implement a strategy
- ✓ How to re-invent yourself
- ✓ I lived it. I did it - Extensive personal experiences
- ✓ Proven tools, techniques and strategies for success
- ✓ Practical tips for effective execution
- ✓ Clear identifiable goals and aims
- ✓ Implementation strategies at all steps
- ✓ Design your own career change plan
- ✓ Identify your strengths and weaknesses
- ✓ Maximize your transferable skills
- ✓ Create your own personal brand
- ✓ Understand how social media will help you
- ✓ Five Step Approach fits all
- ✓ Inspire, motivate and enact
- ✓ Extensive analysis of career needs, attributes, attitudes
- ✓ Identify and implement an action plan for career change success
- ✓ An equal opportunity book that is suitable for all
- ✓ More focused on baby boomers, but useful for all who are contemplating career change

BENEFITS OF THE BOOK FOR YOU:

This book will help, assist, motivate, inspire and provide a step by step structured approach to a very daunting and extremely difficult task – changing careers!

I'm not here to help you write your resume or give you tips on interview technique or tell you what job you should get. I'm here to provide a proven strategy to help guide you through the process that will enable you to make important decisions for your own career choice. A blueprint for career change success.

The Five Step Approach of this book creates a manageable working plan that provides tools, goals, techniques, strategies and personal practical experiences each step of the way. The object is to assist you in overcoming obstacles and barriers and provide direction for the optimal path to career change success.

Certainly some of the book's benefits are:

- ✓ It can make your world simpler and easier to understand
- ✓ Provides options and courses of action
- ✓ Helps remove stress and anxiety
- ✓ Creates purpose and a mission
- ✓ Creates a clear defined structured five step plan of action to focus on
- ✓ Helps you identify what you really want
- ✓ Makes you look closely at your own strengths and weaknesses
- ✓ Provides clarity of purpose
- ✓ Creates a plan of action – gives aim and purpose
- ✓ Identifies tools and strategies
- ✓ Reading another person's career experiences gives a new perspective
- ✓ Relieves stress knowing you have a definitive guide

- ✓ Allows new thoughts and approaches
- ✓ Information is power
- ✓ Identifies choices
- ✓ Makes you think in a positive constructive way
- ✓ Inspires and motivates to take action
- ✓ Identifies and clarifies goals
- ✓ Simplifies the task
- ✓ Helps you get from where you are to where you want to be
- ✓ Creates clarity of thought on a very scary topic

I hope that the contents and experiences in this book help you in YOUR career changing journey.

FIVE STEP APPROACH TO CAREER CHANGE SUCCESS

WHAT DO YOU WANT
(Identify goals)

WHERE ARE YOU NOW
(PRESENT CAREER & LIFE)

WHAT YOU NEED TO HAVE
(STRATEGIES, TOOLS, SKILLS, TECHNIQUES)

HOW TO GET THERE
(Plan of action / Career roadmap)

WHAT YOU NEED TO DO
(Action / Execute)

INTRODUCTION

I always remember that famous saying from the film "Forest Gump" - "Life is like a box of chocolates"... that is so true!

So take what you are given and make the most of it.

Always remember L.I.F.E. – Life is for Enjoying!

BABY BOOMERS!
This book is focused more towards baby boomers than any other segment of the population. However, the steps, principles, information, tools, directives and techniques discussed in this book are applicable to all ages, all economic levels, all races and both sexes... I do not discriminate in trying to help and give direction to changing your career!

I am an equal opportunity book author.

Increasingly, people are being forced to change careers due to business closures and layoffs resulting from many factors. Some have been aware of such changes coming and have anticipated the challenges and obstacles associated with a mid-life change. Some are still wondering what is happening to the world they once knew. For those the obstacles can be numerous and formidable. Decisions have to be made and action needs to be taken. This is the time to take control of the direction you wish your career to go and the focus you must have to succeed.

Changing careers can be a difficult and stressful decision at any time. Career changes can be even more stressful for baby boomers as they are either reaching the height of their career, getting closer to the end of their careers or they have already ended their traditional careers.

Some of the reasons for career changing:

- ✓ The downsizing or restructuring of industries
- ✓ New challenge needed
- ✓ Negative work environment
- ✓ Change needed in your balance of work and life

- ✓ Not appreciated
- ✓ Money and/or benefits not adequate
- ✓ Relocation

According to a recent article nearly fifty percent of people currently employed spend about an hour per day searching for another position.

To succeed in changing your career, one must focus on a number of important things that will help facilitate change:

- ✓ Education and/or skill set
- ✓ Resources to accomplish the task
- ✓ Clear and defined tasks to attain goals
- ✓ Strong determination to achieve goals

Success is in the mind of the beholder. To achieve success it is up to you to make the conscious decision to work for that goal. Everyone's version of success is different. It is up to you to determine what your true goals are and what determines success for you.

Life is more complex, more demanding, more involved, worldlier and more stressful than ever. We have moved from a traditional industrial manufacturing base to the super highway of internet and informational technology of global proportions. This transition has created profound changes in the way we perceive our careers and our society.

Whether it is in your career or your life or both, potential change is on your mind. This book will focus more on career than personal life changes.

This book is written to help guide you through the process of changing your career and provide a career roadmap to assist you on your journey. Ten years ago I was in that very situation. Now I'm in a welcome position of being able to help you with your career potential and help you overcome many of the circumstances and situations you are now facing or are about to face.

I HAVE CHANGED CAREERS MANY TIMES IN MY LIFE
ESPECIALLY SINCE I TURNED FIFTY…
I'VE LIVED IT. I'VE DONE IT!

Introduction | 21

At various points in this book I have highlighted what I did; my risks- my journey. These are personal experiences and events that have shaped my career development over my numerous career changes. Know that you are not alone; that someone has been down that road and is willing to share their experiences with you. The value of this book is found in the information, strategies, tools and helpful directives provided and the wisdom gained from years of practical experience.

---

*"Inform the mind and you may change the mind
But touch the heart and you may change a life"*

I hope I can touch your heart as well as your mind. So follow the book though the Five Step Approach and learn from my experiences as they unfold in each chapter.

I DID IT... SO CAN YOU!

ONCE UPON A TIME
"Once upon a time in a far off land many years ago "... in a pub far away in London, England, I decided my life needed to change - big time!!!

I decided to make bold moves to change the environment I was working in during my mid-twenties. That was 1979... I left England for Los Angeles.

That revelation began a thought process that would lead me to many serious and life changing actions that allowed me to move countries, change careers and change the very fabric of who I was and who I was to become!

I think that can be classed as a major shift!

I hope my opening statement of this book will encourage you to read on because I am "you". I decided that my life and career was not what I wanted it to be, so I decided to change it.

Being in a pub in England is a great place to think or drown your sorrows or both! I had a great education in England, an Honors degree from an excellent university in England and four years of top quality professional training in the accounting and finance world. I was working in a prestigious accounting/finance/consulting firm in London; BUT, my life was empty and I was unhappy doing that kind of work.

England at this time was suffering from an economic malaise and so were many of my colleagues and friends – then one day I said enough, I have to do something! Like everyone in this position it was easy to identify that things were not what I wanted in life and in my career. However, it is so much harder to think about how to change things for the better.

I was in need of an overhaul in both life and career. I felt England could not offer me opportunity. I evaluated my options. I loved travel and adventure so why not go for it... My plan was to go to the USA... land of opportunity and Los Angeles in particular.

If I couldn't make it in the USA, I would try Canada - and if not Canada then down to Australia where I had relatives. That was my PLAN OF OPPORTUNITY. Once that plan had seeded in my head I needed to think practically how I was to do this.

Many aspects of my life needed to be assessed and decisions made. I bought a one way ticket to Los Angeles and arranged to stay with a family for a short time, who I had met in Israel.

I landed in LA and immediately went looking for a job... Any job! I was in LA for about a week when I noticed a job posting in the LA Times newspaper for 20th Century Fox. I went to the Fox human resources department personally and dropped off my resume. The next week in the LA Times was another job posting at MGM.

Somehow, I got interviewed at MGM and 20th Century Fox. How did that happen? I do not clearly remember. I had no film industry experience in Europe; but my education, financial training and being in the right place at the right time, allowed that interview to happen. On the basis of my resume and my interview, 20th Century Fox offered me a job at the studio.

My world suddenly changed!

My approach was get a plan, move forward, make it happen and no going back... a true one way ticket! I was lucky! Right place at the right time. A door opened and I jumped through it.

A bold dramatic move! Most definitely... and it paid off handsomely. At the time, I did not fully realize that the entertainment industry would be my career for the next twenty-five years and would provide me with such fulfillment and happiness.

I will never forget the time in that pub, making the decision that my life, my career had to change! I took action... I made a plan and moved on it.

WHO IS JR
Who is JR? is an amended line from the famous TV series "Dallas". JR also happens to be my initials!

I wrote this book ("Change Your Career... Baby Boomers!" – A Motivational Career Guide), present seminars, speak at events and produced a DVD based on this book, all for one reason – to help people who really want to change their careers.

I am a recognized authority in significant aspects of the Media and Entertainment business with extensive business experience with major companies such as 20th Century Fox and the Summer Olympic Games organization. During my career, I have participated in numerous entrepreneurial business ventures involving world-wide marketing/sales and business consulting in many business sectors.

During my earlier years, I acquired exceptional business training from one of the largest accounting and consulting companies in the world, Touche Ross - their clients included Rolls Royce, General Electric and Chrysler. This training provided a sound base for my many business ventures, including owning my own international media distribution company for many years with clients such as Marvel Comics; Pope John Paul II; O.J. Simpson and Paul Watson - Green Peace founder.

My current career includes being a published book author; motivational speaker; business owner; international entrepreneur; seminar presenter; university lecturer, and of course, being a baby boomer!

Since turning fifty, I have totally re-invented myself. I have documented my struggle to identify what I really wanted; coming to terms with the circumstances; evaluating my options; examining my strengths and weaknesses; understanding the tasks in hand; coping with adversity. With my experiences as a guide, this book will help you be successful in the formidable task of career change.

During the last three years, I have had time to reflect on my journey. What did I do right and what did I do wrong? The result was my decision to write this book. This book documents my successes and trials and tribulations over these last few years, culminating in the emergence of the definitive FIVE Step Approach to career change success.

MY GOAL IS TO HELP PEOPLE, ESPECIALLY BABY BOOMERS, TAKE CONTROL OF THEIR SITUATION AND FIND THE CAREER THEY WANT AND DESERVE.

WHY DID I WRITE THIS BOOK
Ten years ago, I had no career and nowhere to live.

What was I to do and where was I to live?
How did I arrive at my decision process?
How did I address the many fears and problems I had to deal with?
How did I create new careers and new avenues of fulfillment?

A number of important events have happened in the last decade that have significantly impacted my world.

Firstly, technology and negative demand changes in my industry.

Secondly, global competition (globalization) fundamentally changed business and the employment environment.

Thirdly, the financial collapse of 2007, created serious disruption to the "American dream".

These changes and my own personal situation, created a scenario that demanded major changes in my life and career. After years of working through so many questions, situation assessments, decisions and hypotheticals, I found myself in a good place. During this period, I allowed myself to focus on how I managed to be successful in charting the troubled waters of career change and how I might help others in similar situations.

So why did I write this book?

The real answer is I wanted too! Writing a book is a real challenge and I love challenges, so why not!

Secondly, I want this book to help people in need of inspiration and guidance.

I fundamentally believe that this is your life, so live it. Do what you love. If you don't like something, change it. Open your mind. Often opportunities only come once, seize them. Life is short. Live your dream.

Over many years, my good friend Jim Marrinan (an expert in international television programming) and I would regularly meet up in LA or NY. We often discussed career development. Jim would constantly tell me how amazed he was that I was able to re-invent myself as circumstances changed. He encouraged me to share my experiences and exploits with others.

When I wrote my book on the film business ("The Film Biz Bible"), I sent a copy to him and he was so complimentary. Later he asked to use passages from my book to assist him in his business presentation to a client. What an honor!

Jim died in 2012 – a tragedy to me and to many others who treasured him as a true gentlemen, good friend and top professional.

So this book is dedicated to my friend Jim.

WHY THIS BOOK IS DIFFERENT
Prior to starting the process of writing this book, I read many books on the topic of motivation, both in life and career. Certainly, I felt strongly that I wanted my own journey, my life experiences and what career paths I have chosen and why, to be the major contributing factor in this book. I wanted dearly to help and assist people from all walks of life, especially baby boomers, who wanted to change their career by benefiting from my journey.

I needed to provide an in depth study on the many elements that go into decisions and attitudes that affect both your career and life. Very soon the scope of the book expanded considerably. Now this book has many segments on very important topics that will help provide you tools, understanding and techniques that will guide you in your journey – all highlighted by my own experiences and career path decisions.

I reviewed a large number of books on these subjects. A number were good, but many were not "my cup of tea". Many of them were long winded; unclear in their focus; too academic or focused on one specific area of career development. I wish to inspire and motivate others based on my own experiences and by clearly identifying skills, tools, techniques and strategies that will help guide you on your journey. However, you must act and not just act but act in a positive and consistent manner to achieve your goals.

WHAT IS THE MOST IMPORTANT QUESTION
When it comes to having a truly fulfilling and successful career, one important question needs to be addressed.

What do you want?
The need to decide what you want in your career and what you value the most is central to being happy. Without this answer it is difficult to move forward. My book will help you get from where you are in your career, to where you truly want to be. Not just theory, but very practical advice and guidance.

This book will help you:
- ✓ Be positive
- ✓ Define your goals
- ✓ Elevate your self-esteem
- ✓ Elevate your motivation
- ✓ Provide tools to succeed
- ✓ Create confidence
- ✓ Reduce negatives, enhance positives
- ✓ Become proactive
- ✓ Define priorities
- ✓ Make informed decisions
- ✓ Enhance professional relationships
- ✓ Improve your communication skills

- ✓ Learn from failures
- ✓ Help you achieve your defined goals

This book will help and assist you in all these areas! …now let's get on with it!

"Success means having the courage, the determination, and the will to become the person you believe you were meant to be"
George A. Sheehan

WHY NOT YOU

Changing careers is a journey that requires a great deal of fortitude, perseverance and an ability to overcome adversity. Focus on your goals and maintain a clear defined path to achieving those goals.

Just the thought of changing your career can be so daunting that it quickly disappears into the deepest recesses of your mind. What was I thinking to even contemplate changing my career? Such thoughts are perfectly normal. Fear and anxiety are typical reactions to such career changing thoughts.

Many factors come into play when a person contemplates a career change. Some of these factors are obvious such as financial gain or job satisfaction or even having to find a job due to being made unemployed. In my case I was turning fifty and I was faced with a major career dilemma. I did not have a career! I was a man with no career, a ship not just without a rudder, but without a ship!

The statement of "why not you?" has many connotations. I would like to focus on the one that meant the most to me when I was deep into the career change mentality namely, "anything is possible and if others can do it why not me?"

Once you grasp that meaning, your approach becomes more determined and your self-confidence elevates. Suddenly goals become achievable. The "why not me?" seems attainable.

*MOTIVATION * ATTITUDE * INSPIRATION * GOALS DETERMINATION * SELF-ESTEEM * SUCCESS*

These words permeate this book and are so important to you during the journey to help create a positive mindset and that "why not me?" attitude.

We all react differently to situations and those reactions can be positive or can be negative. During the last ten years, since I "re-invented" myself, I have enabled myself to thoroughly evaluate how I react to situations and what my strengths and weakness are, both in career and life.

When the thoughts of a career change occur, they may create a state of high anxiety or excitement or a challenge. Certainly for me ten years ago, I was in a state of "what the heck do I do with my life and especially what do I do for a career"

There was a need to fully evaluate my circumstances and assess my strengths and weaknesses. Embedded into that thought process was a fundamental need for me to decide what I really wanted in a career. The Five Step Approach discussed in this book goes into depth about this process.

All during the process of deciding a course of action and then following it through, **MOTIVATION** was an important feature of my success. Motivation by definition involves the ability to move towards an assigned goal. Motivation helps maintain that focus and drive to achieve your goal.

During the course of my numerous career moves motivation has ebbed and flowed in its intensity; however, there is no doubt that having the ability to self-motivate is critical to your success in career change. Motivation will and does provide a much needed bridge between where you are presently to where you want to be in the future. Motivation provides fuel to keep you going and provides the drive to create the environment for positive action. Without motivation your intimidating journey will be made very difficult.

To achieve career change success, you need to acquire and maintain the ability to be motivated. That means overcoming procrastination, anxiety and fear of your present situation or what might happen in the future.

A major aspect of change is the fear of failure. Be positive and create goals and desires that can be realistically achieved. Create an attitude of optimism and reduce negativity. Focus on a positive outcome and not negative events. Create short-term tasks to achieve long-term goals.

Detailed planning and defined goals will reduce negative thoughts. Overnight success is rare. Motivation is charged by positive results; therefore, action is required to move you in the right direction. Motivation is a critical element of success. Focus on maintaining a good attitude.

What an interesting topic, motivation. I constantly look to be motivated. Anything can help me be motivated. A desire for excellence or even a fear to fail will motivate. A desire to accomplish a goal, a challenge will motivate. Trying something new and pushing that envelope would motivate.

To write a book is a huge challenge and to attempt this new goal was a significant motivator. Focus on the positive, the uplifting. We all need motivation.

My recently deceased friend, Jim Marrinan, whenever we talked, was always uplifting and positive. I always felt after our conversations a feeling of being positive and motivated. Having a peer who gives positive feedback and stimulating thoughts is always an advantage.

Motivation is truly the engine that allows you to continue your journey of career change.

Motivation is a crucial element in setting and attaining goals. Focus on your goals and what you want. Start being who you want to be.

"Desire is the key to motivation, but it's determination and commitment to an unrelenting pursuit of your goal — commitment to excellence — that will enable you to attain the success you seek."

Mario Andretti

ATTITUDE is another career change component that is extremely important.

A positive uplifting attitude that is consistent is so beneficial. It is your choice on what kind of attitude you wish to put forward on a daily basis. A positive attitude creates a "can do" approach. It enables you to be constructive, innovative and productive.

A negative attitude encourages pessimism and is counter-productive.

I am lucky, as I was blessed with having a positive attitude to life and career. I was also a very self-motivated person; however, during the last ten years, at times I have struggled to maintain the levels desired, as events have occurred that have "knocked me down" and deflated my enthusiasm. Such events in life are to be expected.

It is during those times of adversity that the need to have the ability to **PERSEVERE** is strongest. Your ability to remain committed to the task in hand; to focus on the goals you wish to achieve and to ensure you provide the time and effort to achieve those goals, highlights your level of **PERSEVERANCE**. The difference between success and failure might be that extra effort you give to make things happen.

During my career change journey, I can one hundred percent tell you that there were times when I felt dejected, overwhelmed and could not see a positive end to what I wanted to achieve. But, I learned that this is all part of the process and if you continue to fight, you will truly benefit and move forward in a positive manner. The key is perseverance.

No one said changing careers would be easy!

Changing careers, demands a great deal of thought, direction, hard work, motivation, a positive attitude and a great deal of perseverance.

All these attributes were severely tested when I left Los Angeles and moved to a small town of five thousand people in the Olympic Peninsula, two hour's drive west of Seattle.

I moved from the hub of the entertainment world that I had known for over twenty years, to a small rural area in the middle of nowhere!

What was I to do career-wise?

My film and media distribution business was no longer viable. I had to re-invent myself so I could earn a living and also keep myself busy. I sat down to look at what was viable for me and what I really wanted to do.

University teaching (career #6) appealed to me; but, I knew nothing about what it really took to get into that industry and whether I had the credentials to enter it.

It took many months of research, reviewing university websites, calling people and not being deterred by difficulties of accessing information and focusing on the right areas, for me to progress.

Teaching at university was a completely new industry for me and perseverance was a necessity. I learned that to formally teach at a university, a PhD was usually necessary. However, after more research, I found that having a master's degree and having valuable years of business experience in the area you wish to teach can be a major plus. Doors could open for me to become an adjunct professor.

Universities like to have people with extraordinary practical business experience with a minimum of a master's degree. Such a teaching position is classed as an adjunct professor.

At times during this process, I felt like giving up. Too many obstacles to overcome - but each day I kept going... more and more research.

I had to assess my educational credentials to see if they would fit the position. I had an Industrial Economics Bachelor's Degree from an English university. Those credentials would have to be verified. The English university education system is one of the best in the world, but how would that degree rank in the USA regarding teaching credentials?

Secondly, I was trained for four years in finance and accounting for a professional qualification in England. I was told the classes were equivalent to an MBA in the USA. However, how would a university view the credits?

On both questions, I did not know the answers? More research and more obstacles to overcome.

To assist me in overcoming these obstacles, I decided to obtain a USA master's degree to add to my skill set. I decided on a Master's of Science degree.

Once I had obtained the USA master's degree and added that to my other qualifications, I felt ready to approach a university for a teaching position at a University School of Business, Marketing department.

I had to carefully prepare a resume and cover letter that would clearly highlight my skills and attract attention from a university department head. My resume/cover letter had to be attention getting – highlighting my vast business experience, including 20th Century Fox; my training with a worldwide accounting firm; my years at the Olympic Games, and of course, my many years having my own worldwide production and media distribution company.

I had to stand out and make a positive impression. I needed to get an interview. I decided to contact a number of university heads of department in addition to the normal route through the human resource department. I researched all the local universities and directed cover letters/resume to specific university department chairs that had International marketing courses. Once again, I focused on the area I felt I was the strongest at and had the most credentials.

I then waited! A few days later I received a call from the Business Program at the University of Washington, Bothell campus. I had my interview. My first venture into a new industry. I was not sure what to expect.

The lady was a professor in the business program. She was impressed by my extraordinary business background and my educational qualifications met her needs. We discussed a great deal about what I was looking for and what she needed. She had a course on International Marketing available the next quarter and needed a lecturer. It was part-time but it was exactly what I needed to get my foot in the door.

She loved my experience and my quality education background. We discussed the qualities needed to provide a positive teaching experience for the students and the need to adhere to a strict academic catalogue of standards and requirements of a degree course.

What became interesting were her comments about her past experiences with adjunct lecturers who came from the business world. She felt that all to too often, they talked more about business stories and less on the curriculum required for the degree course.

So my perseverance had paid off. After two years of making all those strenuous efforts to understand and meet the requirements, I had finally been offered a lecturer position.

Goal met! I was offered the position subject to my educational qualifications being verified.

It took months to get all my academic records verified. Then the day came for me to walk into a university lecture hall for the first time to teach thirty young and hungry students about International Marketing, part of the students' business degree course.

The whole process took just over two years, from the time I decided I wanted to become a university lecturer as a goal, to achieving that goal!

That journey clearly follows the Five Step Approach of this book and highlights the process required to change your career - it worked for me.

"The difference between a successful person and others is not a lack of strength, not a lack of knowledge, but rather a lack in will"
Vince Lombardi

When making any major steps in your career, there will be barriers, both real and imaginary, standing in your way. What is required is to focus on the barriers that stand in your way and consider ways to erase them in the most economical and practical way. It is human to have self-doubt and feel the task at hand may be too much to overcome. Have confidence and a problem solving mind.

Half the battle is to know the right questions to ask. Finding the answers can be easier than you think. Information is a powerful tool and can often help you overcome barriers and obstacles.

I cannot imagine a more intimidating barrier than entering a new country; trying to set up home and find a job! That was my barrier early in my career in my twenties!

I was leaving the UK and travelling to the USA for a new beginning!

You cannot succeed if you never try.

> "It is hard to fail, but it is worse never to have tried to succeed"
> **Theodore Roosevelt**

Along with motivation, attitude and perseverance, another attribute needed is **INSPIRATION!**

Inspiration can be a significant motivator. It can raise your spirits and your work effort to new heights and create a positive environment. We all need a level of inspiration. The ability of a person from lowly beginnings to become the President of the United States or a person that excels beyond reason or the ability of a person to write a song that touches you is truly inspiring. Your ability to be inspired, to be motivated and to persevere allows you to feel "WHY NOT YOU?".

Inspiration is a necessity. I have seen and met many people who have inspired me. My own inspirational thoughts have propelled me to develop ideas and courses of action that have significantly helped my personal and career development.

I love to see and hear inspirational stories of success. I'm sure you are aware of many yourself. Use them to motivate and inspire you.

I have been in places of amazing creativity (on the set of the TV series "MASH") or at the summer Olympic Games watching the best athletes perform above and beyond – truly inspirational!

> "Life is not measured by the number of breathes we take, but by the moments that take our breath away."
> **George Carlin**

Career change can be and often is scary and intimidating. It can cause a person not to act, to hesitate, to fear change. We all have the ability to **PROCRASTINATE.**

It is so easy to put off important tasks and yet complete a relatively meaningless unimportant task. We are all guilty of putting off decisions. Where career change is required and important decisions are needed, procrastination is often present.

Procrastination is one of the very best ways to avoid success and not achieve your goals. People procrastinate for many different reasons. When it leads to decisions being put off or not made at all, the consequences for inaction can be extremely negative. At some point you will need to recognize this situation and address the issues. Once addressed, a well thought out informed plan can be put in effect.

I too have been afflicted by the procrastination disease! Many years ago in London, it took me eight pints of beer a night, a boring job and a screwed up marriage to finally get me to act – and move to USA!

If you manage to avoid procrastinating and get a task done the feeling of accomplishment is so positive and uplifting. I can list so many tasks that the urge to just stop and avoid doing them was upper most in my mind; but you must be strong and motivated. Create motivation and follow through.

We all suffer from procrastination. We are human. Your ability to overcome and move forward is a quality that must be mastered. The ability to push through and continue working on a task even though you want to find any excuse not to, is required.

"Successful and unsuccessful people do not vary greatly in their abilities. They vary in their desires to reach their potential"
John Maxwell

It is interesting to observe, that if all the attributes previously mentioned - namely, motivation, attitude, perseverance and inspiration are all functioning properly, a person will likely have a healthy amount of **SELF-ESTEEM** and **SELF-CONFIDENCE.**

What an interesting topic! A topic that goes to the very core of who we are! This topic is one of the most talked about and discussed topics. Everyone has an opinion. There is one thing that we all agree is that our self-esteem has significant ramifications in all facets of our life and career.

Self-esteem is created on the building blocks of success.

Success in life; success with people; success with relationships; success with career, tends to lead to high levels of self-esteem. Esteem and success often go hand in hand as does the opposite. Little success usually leads to low self-esteem. It is important to forgive yourself for your mistakes; take credit for your successes and do not focus on your weakness, but highlight your strengths. Be positive in your attitude and minimize lack of self- confidence.

Creating and possessing self-confidence and positive self-esteem is a core building block for career change success.

There is no doubt that having success helps your self-esteem/self-confidence and similarly, having failures diminishes your self-esteem.

A personal revelation for me, was how much I enjoyed teaching at university (career #6) and realizing that my level of confidence and exceptional knowledge on the subject I was teaching was significant.

They say that to teach a subject you really need to fully understand and know what you are teaching. That is one hundred percent right. That revelation gave me a huge boost in my self-esteem.

Writing a book about the business aspects of the independent film industry gave me major satisfaction and a huge boost in my self-esteem. To write a book was one of my life goals and to complete that task was amazing.

If other people can do it and have done it, then so can you! Therefore, "WHY NOT YOU?" applies to you as much as anyone else.

Let this book be the catalyst to motivate and inspire you to move forward, help create a template for change and take the steps to a rewarding and positive new career.

BEING A BABY BOOMER!

WHO ARE BABY BOOMERS
Boomers are generally recognized as born between 1946 and 1964. That's me!

There are seventy million boomers, some twenty-eight percent of the population. The average baby boomer male has had three or four different careers and has been employed by at least four different companies.

This significant population bubble has created major impacts in all levels of industry and society as the boomers marched through the ageing process. The economic and social impact of boomers has been truly amazing. Boomers have generally been career focused with a strong motivation to succeed. Boomers have felt the full impact of television and the exposure to advertising, commercial exploitation and materiality.

Due to advances in medical and general health considerations boomers will live significantly longer than past generations. Extending the working life means learning how to adjust to the new environment. Such a new market of opportunities allows boomers to exploit new avenues in their careers, relying on their own ingenuity, skills and experience.

A recent survey states that a significant number of baby boomers, unlike their parents, plan to work in retirement. They need continued income and they want greater flexibility in retirement employment avenues. Boomers are re-inventing what the later years of life are all about and the way retirement is perceived.

WAKE UP CALL
The world has changed significantly over the last decade. These changes have and are continuing to significantly affect the mood and attitude of baby boomers as they approach the latter stages of their working life.

Wake up call #1: America's traditional ideas of retirement are fundamentally changing.

Wake up call #2: The financial collapse of 2007 created major disruption in business and employment.

Wake up call #3: Significant changes in technology and global competition have changed the employment landscape.

Wake up call #4: Financial security is no longer assured.

Wake up call #5: Employment security is no longer assured.

Wake up call #6: The "American Dream" has been seriously depleted.

What does all this mean to baby boomers and how do you overcome the concerns and obstacles with regards to our own career?

YOUR skills, YOUR abilities, YOUR experience, YOUR wisdom will propel you forward.

Follow my... "FIVE STEP APPROACH TO CAREER CHANGE SUCCESS"

CAREER OPTIONS
I personally have had to address these circumstances and evaluate my options as a maturing baby boomer. This book is a direct result of my journey through this process and my journey continues today.

What are the career options?

Remain where you are?
Many boomers will and do consider remaining in their current position and maintaining their present career path. This option may be the correct approach, as many baby boomers have attained success in their present position and further promotions may be possible. Job security and family commitments are a major priority regarding career decision making.

Retire?
The ability to retire and have financial security can and still is a viable option, providing it has been planned and organized in advance. Based on recent research that situation is not always an option for many boomers. The American dream and the ability to retire and live comfortably have taken a significant down turn in

recent years. Even if retirement is an option many boomers wish to continue working in some form.

New Opportunities?

Times they are a changing! For many of the reasons we have discussed, there comes a point in the life of a boomer where circumstances, or just a strong desire for a significant career change, has arrived. After following a traditional career path for many years the time has come to re-evaluate and find a different path, whether it be a true passion, just a change or economic necessity. A career change of such significance demands careful evaluation and a strong commitment to succeed.

Changing career course in later life can be overwhelming! It is a fact that baby boomers have grown up in a society where the norm was to get an education, find a job with a strong company, then have enough money to sustain their way of life in retirement. Circumstances have changed.

Changing careers can create fear and uncertainty; however, there is also the view that much can be gained and benefits reaped in the new world order we find ourselves in. A major career change requires thought, focus, adaptability, new skills, determination and guidance.

We "boomers" comprise twenty-eight percent of the US population and total over seventy million people. Such a force creates a strong economic block. This is a potentially highly beneficial employment scenario!

As we have progressed through the various stages of life, the economic impact of boomers has been seriously felt in all levels of the economic strata. Major industries have grown and developed to service our needs. Now boomers are moving into their maturing years, new and old industries will make every effort to fulfill our needs.

Take advantage of your skills and experience and focus on new opportunities that will expand or create new services for the needs of many millions of maturing baby boomers. Opportunities are and will be created – move forward into new careers.

GOLDEN OPPORTUNITY

Acknowledge the time has arrived as new businesses are created and expanded to service the needs of millions of maturing baby boomers. There is truly a GOLDEN OPPORTUNITY for baby boomers to find new careers and new ventures.

It is estimated that more than eighty percent of baby boomers (who will, on average, live to be eighty-three years old) plan to keep working after retirement. Such a situation creates amazing opportunities – older people will continue to work way after retirement age. We're all living in a very different world than what we grew up in. It's the great re-invent.

It is highly likely that boomers, instead of retiring, will be starting new businesses and working to finance their future. Many of these will be downsizing, not just their houses, but everything about their lifestyle. Lifestyle shifts as well as career shifts will and are happening.

A new poll finds three-fourths of all baby boomers consider themselves only middle-aged or younger, and that includes most of the boomers who are ages fifty-seven to sixty-five. One-fourth of boomers feel you're not old until you're eighty or older.

This boomer attitude and the realization of an economic and employment new order will create a whole new environment for many millions of boomers. Baby boomers may not want to do the same type of work after fifty years old that they did when they were younger. More than fifty percent of working retirees say they want to work in a new field.

Baby boomers have much to offer the workforce, whether as full-time employees, part-timers, consultants or in other innovative work arrangements. Some statistics have shown that more than fifty percent of U.S. companies are willing to negotiate special arrangements for older workers just to keep them in the workplace. What are these new expanding needs and services?

With the influx of many millions of people into later life, whole new industries will spring up, plus industries presently functional will require large expansions to cater for boomer needs. There are a number of industry sectors that are creating new opportunities such as in healthcare, assisted living, education, government, consulting, leisure activities, travel, social media, consulting, technology and, of course, starting your own business in any sector is an obvious avenue.

A new brand of entrepreneurs has been created based on the needs of maturing baby boomers. This new environment will create many new self-employed businesses for boomers. The number of "self-employed" incorporated businesses has risen nearly twenty-five percent over the past decade. Boomers are also creating careers in social media and other technologies. The fifty-five to sixty-five year old demographic base has the highest rate of entrepreneurship in the US.

It is a fact, that baby boomers also have significant disposable income, free time, skill and experience to try new activities. There are so many industry sectors that will benefit by the boomer economic impact.

Instead of moving into full-time retirement, boomers are investing savings and starting businesses. Boomers are competing with young graduates for opportunities and are focused on learning new skills and opening up new opportunities.

Doom and gloom or a new age of opportunity?
This is the new reality! The second half of your life can be a time of a new awareness through new and diverse career choices.

What challenges are ahead and how will you approach these career changes?

MY CAREERS

I have been through a number of career changes, some by my choice, some caused by circumstances beyond my control. The following outlines my career changes in my life to-date. This will provide an insight into my wide and varied working life.

Please take note of the number of careers I have had and the different countries I had to deal with. It is interesting to see a common thread, but also see the diversity of occupations and the development and skills transferred during my career.

Take note of my life and career moves in the last ten years from 2003 to 2013. These years were very dramatic in my life, as I realized the full impact of being a maturing baby boomer and what being a boomer really meant in terms of career challenges.

CAREER #1 (Accounting phase)
- Location: London, England
- Large Accounting/Financial Professional Firm – Touche Ross
- Position: Professional Chartered Accountant
- Training: Four years of intense professional training

CAREER #2 (Major Film Studio phase)
- Location: Los Angeles, USA
- Company: 20th Century Fox
- Term: Four years
- Position: Executive in TV division
  Controller, Fox Sports

CAREER #3 (Olympic Games phase)
- Location: Los Angeles, USA
- Company: LAOOC – Los Angeles Olympic Games
- Term: Two years
- Position: VP Controller

CAREER #4 (Europe phase)
- Location: London, England
- Company: Touche Ross. Large consulting firm
- Term: One year
- Position: Chief Media Consultant

CAREER #5 (Indie Film phase)
- Location: Los Angeles, USA; Zurich, Switzerland
- Company: Film production & distribution worldwide
- Term: Fifteen years
- Position: President and owner
- Note: Acquired Masters in Science degree.

BABY BOOMER PERIOD: 2003 (just turned fifty) – To present

CAREER #6 (University Professor phase)
- Location: Miami & Seattle, USA
- University of Miami – School of Business
  School of Communication
  University of Washington, Bothell - Business Program
- Term: Six years (2003 – 2009)
- Position: UM: Full-time adjunct professor (Marketing)
  UW: Part-time adjunct professor (Marketing)

CAREER #7 (Author; Seminar Presenter; Producer; Social Media; Speaker phase) *Comprised three phases:*

PHASE #1: Film Seminars; Film Book Author
- Created personal brand "Mr. Film Biz"; marketed brand on Facebook; LinkedIn; Meetups etc.
- Created Mr. Film Biz website (www.mrfilmbiz.com)
- Created a two day "Film Business" seminar and webinar
- Wrote and published book on the film business - "The Film Biz Bible"

PHASE #2: Film Production – Feature Film "Serenity Farm"
- Produced, marketed and distributed a low budget feature film – thriller suspense (www.serenityfarmthemovie.com)

PHASE #3: Speaker; Author; Business Entrepreneur
- Wrote and published motivational book, Five Step Approach for baby boomers changing careers – "Change Your Career... Baby Boomers!"
- Created personal brand as speaker for Changing Careers... Baby Boomers

- Created website to market speaker and book (www.johnrodsett.com)
- Extensive research into social media for marketing
- Created faith based products company (www.popesainthood.com)

As you can see, not only have I changed careers but I've changed countries and cultures. I have moved from large companies to being self-employed. Add to that list, a significant move from a major city to a small rural area and you get the idea of my journey.

Pay particular attention to Careers #6 and #7 in 2003. I was fifty and my old career had ended. I needed to find a new focus and new location.

I followed my FIVE STEP APPROACH from 2003 to present and will continue using the five steps into the future.

I LIVED IT. I DID IT... following my Five Step Approach!

Some personal thoughts about those career moves:

Career #1... was my first career out of university in England and I moved to London. I went into it because it paid well and it gave me a profession. I hated it!

Career #2 & #3... left England and moved to the USA. Changed my life for the better!

Career #4... was necessary for family reasons and I hated it. However, being back in Europe allowed me to make relationships that would benefit me in the future.

Career #5... was my most rewarding and satisfying career and lasted over fifteen years.

From this period on, I felt the full effects of being a person who was facing major changes, both in my life and in my career, as I was moving into the later stages of my working career.

Career #6... was a major change in career orientation and provided huge satisfaction and pride.

Career #7... is still happening - but again a major change in career orientation that to-date is and will continue to bring me a great deal of satisfaction.

As you read through this book, I continually refer to my experiences, in varying degrees of detail, with each career change; how they came about; how I evaluated each move; each decision; the successes; the frustrations and failures, I encountered. I hope these excerpts from my life career experiences will benefit you.

> "Find out what you like doing best and get someone
> to pay you for doing it."
> **Katherine Whitehorn**

THE NEW WORLD CAREER ORDER

YOU NEED TO BE AWARE OF THIS & UNDERSTAND IT

The world as we have known it for many decades, regarding employment opportunities, has fundamentally changed.

The shift we are discussing involves business, employment and careers. Very little of today's business world resembles the market of a decade ago.

The old established idea of being educated in a specific field; looking for a job in a large company; gaining promotion; job security; increased salary and benefits, has markedly altered.

It's hard to imagine what has actually happened, especially if you are on that ladder and you were brought up in this linear way of career thinking. Certainly, college graduates are facing this new reality in no uncertain manner. People of all ages have to face this change and in many cases it is a frightening wake-up call.

Many industries, jobs and skills have vanished and new skill requirements have replaced them. Old ways of job hunting, resume presentation, job searches and networking have substantially altered – the old ways are no longer viable. New skill sets and new approaches must be adopted and a new attitude to these changes must be accepted.

Many factors have contributed to this significant shift, such as globalization and significant technology advancements. As the world economies become more connected they have increased opportunity, but also increased competition. Add to this, the financial collapse of 2007 and the resulting economic downturn and unemployment, the impact has been serious. The world of employment appears to be moving to short-term contract type employment that is constantly being reviewed with limited benefits and limited security – truly a new world order!

Because of recent events, the employment situation has changed dramatically for many people, especially for baby boomers. This has caused significant anxiety and self-doubt about where they want to go and where they might find themselves.

This shift includes movement from the old philosophy to a new way of thinking in the employment marketplace:

The old traditional approach:
Work to pay the bills
Work is your duty
Work till you retire

The new career approach:
Work has to be more than just a pay check
Work has to have meaning
Work has to be enjoyed

There is a need to explore new avenues. The world of the internet and social media should become a major asset for your future. New circumstances means new approaches.

The ability to re-invent yourself and update your skills is paramount. There is a constant need to be focused on generating potential new opportunities. A need to ensure you are building a network of skills and opportunities on a continuing basis.

With change comes new opportunities, as well as challenges.

The old traditional career approach is no longer valid. Short-term, multiple careers are in.

Full-time and life-time employment has been replaced by short-term, part-time, contract, task specific employment.

Employment security has gone. There are no guarantees of employment or income!

Skill set. The days of having a limited skill set is out. The need to expand and add new skills is critical. Technology proficiency, computer skills and social media knowledge are necessities. Constantly upgrading skills is required.

You are your own boss! The company will no longer look after you. You need to examine yourself, evaluate, and decide what is best for you and then go do it. YOU, YOU and YOU... all three of YOU... you are it! You need to invest in YOU.

Social media is in! You need to ensure that you have created a comprehensive network of contacts and clients via the world of the internet, social media and websites. Focus on LinkedIn, Meetups, Facebook, Twitter, blogs and community groups.

You need to be flexible, focused and entrepreneurial in your attitude to your career. Be pro-active. The new world order is global and very competitive.

Years ago, I read that the Apple founder, Steve Jobs, stated "Do what you love". That statement resonated in me and I was lucky enough to find an industry I loved (entertainment industry). But, how do you find that and how do you know? It all begins with a willingness to acknowledge that you are responsible for your career. Only you can attain the goals you want to set. The task of wanting to change your career and actually doing it can be formidable.

My Five Step Approach to Career Change Success will provide you with the framework and support required to make these changes and attain your goals.

"The tragedy in life doesn't lie in not reaching your goal.
The tragedy lies in having no goal to reach"
Benjamin E. Mays

THE FIVE STEP APPROACH TO CAREER CHANGE SUCCESS

It is your ability to make decisions that will generate action that leads to change. Once you have made that career altering decision you must act - otherwise those thoughts remain thoughts.

Not to act means there is no change.

THE FIVE STEP APPROACH

TO GET FROM WHERE YOUR ARE TO WHERE YOU WANT TO BE

STEP 1: WHAT DO YOU WANT

STEP 2: WHERE ARE YOU NOW

STEP 3: WHAT YOU NEED TO HAVE

STEP 4: HOW TO GET THERE

STEP 5: WHAT YOU NEED TO DO

THE FIVE STEP APPROACH

STEP 1: WHAT DO YOU WANT
You need to identify your goals.

STEP 2: WHERE ARE YOU NOW
Take a long, serious look at your career and where you are heading.

STEP 3: WHAT YOU NEED TO HAVE
To accomplish your goals requires the right tools, strategies, skills and techniques.

STEP 4: HOW TO GET THERE
Create a plan of action, a career roadmap, to help you attain those goals.

STEP 5: WHAT YOU NEED TO DO
You need to act and execute the plan.

Each STEP has its own chapter with experiences, tools and techniques. Each chapter will provide a valuable and practical guide for your journey of change.

"The only way to do great work is to love what you do. If you haven't found it yet, keep looking. Don't settle."
Steve Jobs

"Doubt kills more dreams than failure ever will"
Karim Seddik

STEP 1: WHAT DO YOU WANT
(Identify Goals)

WHAT IS THE MOST IMPORTANT QUESTION
To be able to identify what you really want in your career is very critical. If you feel a disconnect between what you are doing now and what you feel you really want to do - then it's time to re-evaluate and ask that one important question!

What do you want?
Such a simple question; however, this question has huge ramifications. The answer to this question will provide the cornerstone for everything that matters to you.

What you want, your dreams and desires, has to be tempered by realism.

Being a baby boomer provides you with many years of experiences that can assist you in clearly identifying what works and doesn't work for you. This knowledge will help you in your own self-analysis that is required to help you on your career changing journey.

Ask yourself these questions:
- ✓ **Do you know exactly what you want from your career?**
- ✓ **Can you truly identify your goals, desires and ambitions?**
- ✓ **Are you happy and satisfied with your career?**
- ✓ **Are you as financially strong as you need and want to be?**
- ✓ **Are you living the life you really want and having the career you really want?**

Each person is unique; therefore your needs, desires and ambitions are different. It is up to you to make decisions and find for yourself what you really want.

What do you want? ...is not an easy question to answer.
Most people have not really thought about this question. Many stumble through life without real thought or purpose.

A ship without a rudder! ...Does that sound familiar?

Identifying what you want is not easy and requires a great deal of thought and soul searching. It is necessary to focus on the right goals for you. Your goals are unique to you and only you can uncover them. Knowing what you truly want is the single most important question you need to answer to your satisfaction.

"Commitment leads to action. Action brings your dream closer"

Believe me, to thoroughly evaluate yourself is not the easiest task I've ever had in my life. What's more, as I have become older, I feel I've had to re-evaluate myself far more often.

When I decided to leave England for the USA many years ago, I had made the decision that England was not for me and career #1 (accounting/finance) was not making me happy.

I wanted a new challenge, a new adventure. My desire to see what a new country had to offer was, in my opinion, better than what I had going in England.

My goal was simply to go to the New World...
Land of opportunity... The USA.

I had a great university degree and professional training in accounting and finance, so I felt I had a basis on which I could provide value to a new employer in a new country, in a new career.

I felt I had more idea what I didn't want, than what I did want. I was unhappy in the accounting/finance profession and unhappy with the UK. I decided to do something about it.

When you leave your home country and enter another country you face many obstacles, least of which is immigration. If the USA could not provide me with opportunities I planned to go to Canada, and if that didn't work out I would go to Australia, where I had family.

That was my plan of action. My goal was to get into the USA and work and deal with career and life once I was in the USA.

This strategy was not exactly textbook and it had many perilous steps. I do not recommend this course of action because I was incredibility lucky on many fronts and many circumstances fell into place that helped me.

BUT... if you don't act and take a chance you will not get the rewards. I took the chance and the rewards were beyond my wildest dreams.

EXAMINE YOUR CAREER
Part of your evaluation is to focus on your career and identify what path you wish to follow. This process is easier said than done.

What are your goals?
What are your goals in your career? What do you really want and what kind of career do you want? Everyone is different. Goals over time will change; but, it is important to begin this process of what's important to you and what you want in a career.

This is no easy task. Only you can ultimately make those specific goals. What career path will help you accomplish those goals? These are fundament questions that need to be addressed.

What is your dream career?
Most people have not really thought in any depth about this question. They let life dictate their path rather than taking control of their own destiny. The ideal scenario is to find a career that combines what you love to do with what you are great at doing!

Once again, I find myself talking about what I didn't want, rather than what I did want.

When I was young, I realized that my early career was not the career I wanted. I was very unhappy and unfulfilled. I had no idea what career was potentially good for me. I wish I had some guidance then in a similar manner to this book.

What changed my whole life was finding an industry that excited me and gave me huge job satisfaction and motivation to do well. The entertainment industry became my career lifeline and that industry provided me everything I needed in a career.

I found the film industry by being in the USA and applying to 20th Century Fox – career #2. The whole scenario happened by me being in the right place, at the right time for the right position! A sequence of events and timing that truly changed my life.

From the moment I entered the entertainment industry, I found the passion, drive, motivation and desire, I was so lacking in England.

What are your skills, talents?
Identify your skill set. What are you naturally good at?

What are your values?
Your values should be in harmony with your career choice.

What is ideal for you?
Do you prefer fast-paced, constantly changing pressure work environment or does a slow-paced, less stress work environment suit your personality?

This process will not happen overnight. Allow this process to develop over time, it will help clarify your goals and help guide you along a career road that is best suited for you.

Another major career milestone happened to me some twenty years later, after working at 20th Century Fox, the Olympic Games and having my own film company. I decided to move away from Los Angeles - move away from the center of my entertainment universe!

I realized my career and life, as I had known it for over twenty years, was about to change. I had decided to leave LA. The independent film industry I was so successful in for many years, was changing and not for the good. My small independent film company was being slowly squeezed out, as the video boom had declined significantly. Revenues were shrinking dramatically and I was feeling burnt out living in LA.

A major career evaluation was required.
Careers #1, 2, 3, 4 and 5 had passed. Now what?

In a chapter of this book (MY CAREER AFTER FIFTY) I go into considerable depth on my careers after fifty years old – career #6 and career #7.

The end of career #5 signaled a whole new chapter for me, as I realized I was now a maturing baby boomer, and my life was changing materially.

I needed to fully evaluate what skills I had; what values were most important to me; where did I want to live; in what new career I would find happiness. At this time, the world was changing on many fronts (new career world order) and I needed to make major changes to virtually every facet of my life and career.

Those changes included, but were not limited to:

- ✓ *What do I want to do?*
- ✓ *Where do I want live?*
- ✓ *How do I earn money?*

Remember, I owned my own company for many years, so when your own company is no longer doing well you need to adjust, and as I was burnt out being in LA, moving seemed a logical idea. My situation demanded some serious thought.

I had to weigh many factors, one of which was where to live. I looked at many locations and found the Pacific Northwest rather lovely and much more economical to live there.

Next, I had to think about what career interested me and excited me. I was still involved in film, but on a limited basis. I looked at all my skills and talents and realized how much fun it would be to teach at a university, especially in the Marketing and Global Business area.

I knew I would be a great lecturer, plus I was well educated and had great business experience. I thought I would have a chance at getting a part-time adjunct university lecturer position. This whole process took me months and months of research and self-evaluation. I looked at my strengths. I looked at what would make me happy. I knew I had a lot to offer students - both academically and valuable practical business experience. Real world experience!

I knew I wanted to work for myself. Being a university lecturer allows a great deal of self-autonomy. If you are doing a good job, no one bothers you. As an adjunct professor and being part-time, meant I did not participate in all the university bureaucracy. That was perfect for me. So many positives.

I felt that I would get a great deal of job satisfaction from teaching young eager university students. However, the question was, would they allow me to teach without a PHD and no direct university teaching experience?

There was only one way to find out. Luckily for me I found the right Professor at UW who was willing to give me an interview. We met and I was hired to teach a class (five credits) in the upcoming quarter in International Marketing, part of the Business degree program.

What an amazing opportunity! I studied the curriculum and ensured I was proficient in all the academic aspects of the course. I then added examples of my own business experiences to the class to highlight different sections of the curriculum. For many weeks, I taught the class – a new career was born! I enjoyed it so much, even though it was stressful at times. More to do with wanting to do a great job and help those students get the best I could offer.

At the end of the quarter the students are required to hand in confidential evaluations of the quality of your teaching performance. I was told by faculty that I did extremely well and that the students rated me very highly. I cannot tell you the feelings of elation and happiness I got from hearing that evaluation. I got so much job satisfaction from that whole process.

What's interesting is that student evaluations are an important teaching credential, as it basically validates me as an excellent university lecturer in International Marketing. That validation acts as a passport to gain other teaching posts. I passed the test and did really well.

I now had the ability to move forward as a qualified and tested university adjunct professor with a credential from a major university (University of Washington, Bothell) in the USA.
A new career for me was born! (career #6)

"The only thing that stands between you and your dream is the will to try and the belief that it is actually possible"

Joel Brown

WHY A CAREER CHANGE

The average person can expect to change careers several times in their lifetime. What circumstances would cause an individual to potentially change careers?

Many aspects of life will change over time; whether it is financial, family, health, location – things change! Economies and businesses change. Recently economic downturns have significantly affected business in a negative way and the knock on effect is to detrimentally affect the employment market.

It is not uncommon, that people find that a career no longer presents a challenge; is no longer fulfilling; has limited financial rewards or job stress is too much. A career change can and often does need to happen.

> *"Never mistake activity for achievement."*
> **John Wooden**

YOU ARE UNIQUE!

You are unique! No one has what you have; in the way you have it; in the quantities you have it or in the way you manage it!

Only you can do what is necessary to make you happy. No one else can do that for you. You control your own destiny and you can make things happen or not!

Your life. Your responsibility. Your choice. Your goals.
If you chose to have goals, those goals will be unique to you... Your own personal goal DNA!

Focus your attention on where you want to go and what you want to be. Do you need to identify goals in your career? Generally, we don't allocate much time for such thoughts.

Set your goals
Goal setting is a powerful exercise to help provide direction. The process enables you to focus on your future and turn those plans and goals into action.

Setting goals is an important part of the Five Step Approach To Career Change Success. By clearly identifying goals you can focus on what needs to be done. Clarity of thought and clarity of purpose will ensure you keep your focus. Goals provide assistance to identify what needs to be done.

Typical characteristics of goal setting are:

- ✓ Goals can be long-term and short-term
- ✓ Large goals need to be cut into smaller manageable goals
- ✓ Goals need to be specific and attainable
- ✓ Goals should be allocated a time frame

No matter your age or experience setting goals is critical. It provides focus on a path and gives direction on what needs to be done and activities that are required. It helps separate what's important from what's irrelevant and provides motivation and self-esteem based on the successful achievement of goals.

Career objectives provide a framework to define your ideal path. Without these goals, there is no direction, no purpose and no destination. Goals and career objectives allow you to focus your energies on an end result. Having goals can enable a person to identify specific tasks or steps that need to be accomplished along the way in order to reach the desired destination.

Your career DNA and your goals are the starting point for creating a roadmap. Once you have defined a set of goals, then you need to determine what intermediate steps are necessary to achieve that goal. Career goals are important objectives in your future life. It is also important to realize that goals and career objectives need to be regularly reviewed and updated.

Goals can often be a mix of long-term and short-term, as well as specific and general. Long-term goals tend to be more general, since circumstances may change over time, while short-term ones are more specific, since they can be planned for more easily.

When setting objectives or tasks, it's important to consider what is required to achieve those goals. A time frame for achieving the objective that includes regular milestones and self-evaluation is required.

Obstacles are to be expected. If obstacles become unsurmountable then re-evaluate your approach. Flexibility is a positive, rigidity is not.

Career Goals
Career goals should be specific, measurable, clear, focused and achievable. Goals should be written down and open to revision and review. Priorities need to be established and goals identified as long-term or short-term.

I provide many examples in my book of goal setting from my own experiences. I constantly update my larger goals; and, therefore, I have to adjust my smaller goals. An example of goal setting is writing this book.

The large goal is to write a book. Such a large goal has to be broken down into manageable segments. First, I needed to decide which topics I planned to cover in my book. That alone is a goal. I spent weeks going over many topics I wanted to cover and I spent many hours working on topic formats that best worked for me.

Once I defined my chapters, I then worked on each chapter contents. As you can see, I break down a major goal into component smaller goals. In that way I achieve my overall goal. Organization and vision are a must in this process.

Achieving your goals, no matter how small is a success. Your successes will help generate a positive environment for your future endeavors. Each successful step helps create self-confidence and moves you towards the next step.

As you progress through the steps and achieve a goal, no matter how small or large, review your plan and look at the steps to follow.

What is important to you?
As you prepare your new career goals ensure you always are clear about what is important to you.

- ✓ What do you want?
- ✓ What are you good at?
- ✓ What will make you happy?
- ✓ What balance do you look for between career and family?

DECISIONS

The most important decision is the decision that you want a change in your career.

Second most important decision is a change to what.

Third is that you and only you, must identify your goals.

Being indecisive can create an environment of inaction, doubt and complacency. Decisions allow you to control your future. Decide what to focus on. Decide on what is important to you. Your success is all about decisions, attitude, determination and perseverance.

During your decision making process your most valuable personal assets are:

>Your time
>Your knowledge
>Your experience
>Your expertise

These qualities are unique to you and should be fully utilized and maximized to fulfill your goals. You control your career path.

If you do not know where you are going, how do you get there? Defining your goals is the starting point of your success.

"Challenges are what make life interesting and overcoming them is what makes life meaningful."

Joshua J. Marine

In the chapter, MY CAREER, I identified seven career changes.

I had moved from England to the USA, then back to England and then returned back to USA during that long time period.

I have discussed the first five of my careers:

>*Career #1 (Accounting/Finance)*
>*Career #2 (20th Century Fox)*
>*Career #3 (Olympic Games)*
>*Career #4 (Consulting)*
>*Career #5 (Indie Film)*

Moving on from career #5 and being fifty years old meant major changes to my life and my future.

Once I decided to leave Los Angeles and move away from the capital of the film industry, an industry I had been in for most of my adult life, I realized major changes were needed in my life. A thorough evaluation of what I wanted to do and how I was to do it was required.

I had to basically create my own goal DNA (career #6) and that DNA looked something like this:

- ✓ *I enjoyed working for myself*
- ✓ *Wanted to move away from LA*
- ✓ *Wanted a business that can operate anywhere in the world*
- ✓ *Had to fully evaluate my strengths and weaknesses*
- ✓ *Wanted to infuse people with my knowledge and wisdom to help their careers*
- ✓ *Wanted to inspire people and contribute to their success*

In the section Career Evaluation, I describe at length, my decision to make a career change, move from Los Angeles and begin a new career (career #6) to be a university lecturer. These decisions were happening in the later period of my working life.

Personal and career growth
How many people do you know who complain about their job or career? We all need growth, fulfillment, challenges and a sense of appreciation in our life.

Money!
Financial considerations are always important in any goal discussion; however, goals need to be set that are realistic and manageable. Focus on your passion, rewards will follow as you will no doubt shine in your career.

FIND THE INDUSTRY, THEN THE JOB
Try to find an industry you love and then find a job in that industry. If you find an industry you like and have passion and commitment for, you will naturally excel in that environment.

I thought I would include this section because in my case it was very true. I found an industry I loved and flourished in… the entertainment industry. I found it by accident and was in the right place at the right time, with the right credentials and experience.

To have a professional position with opportunity to develop in a company of such stature as 20th Century Fox – what more could I ask for? (career #2)

I often give advice to young people that if you are really interested in an industry, go and find a position in that industry. Your desire, drive and motivation will shine through because you love the industry. Every morning your work environment stimulates you and drives you to excel in your job. Find a way into that industry and your natural enthusiasm for the industry will help you get the right position and move forward up the ladder of success.

"Build your own dreams or someone else
will hire you to build theirs."
Tony A. Gaskins Jr.

BE HAPPY
Work hard, get job promotions and you will be happy!
Is that really true?

In our culture we are conditioned to believe that we need success first and happiness will follow. Happiness and a positive optimism can and does fuel achievement and better performance.

Happiness fuels success, not the other way around.

Cultivating a positive happy attitude creates a motivated and productive person which ultimately leads to positive results.

To focus on negatives is counter-productive. The need to focus on small manageable goals will help alleviate those negative emotions. Once the small goals can be met, then the larger goals come more into focus and become more achievable.

Here are some meaningful thoughts:

> *Think Less, Feel More*
> *Frown Less, Smile more*
> *Talk Less, Listen More*
> *Judge Less, Accept More*
> *Watch Less, Do More*
> *Complain Less, Appreciate More*
> *Fear Less, Love More*

A recent survey listed the "happiest" countries. Factors taken into consideration and rated highly in the survey were economic prosperity, health system, social support network and amount of leisure time.

DENMARK was number one and the USA was way down the order!

> "There is only one person who could ever make you happy, and that person is you"
>
> **David D. Burns**

SELF-EMPLOYED OR EMPLOYEE

To be employed or self-employed poses an interesting question. Many factors contribute to an answer. Which of those states do you prefer? Both have pros and cons.

As boomers reach the latter part of their working life, being self-employed has become an inviting option for many

Benefits: Freedom; no bosses; your own schedule; you keep the money; you are responsible; no excuses; the challenge; you know everything; relationships; work at home

Concerns: Risky; stressful; lonely; long hours; need to do everything

Other areas: Salary; vacations; health insurance; work schedule

There are many books written on this subject. The need to evaluate all aspects before a decision is made to move from one career path to another, especially as drastic as moving from employed to self-employed or vice versa, is required.

I was brought up to expect to work in a corporate world for a big company. My university degree was in Industrial Economics. The best students were hired by the big accounting firms in London. In England it is the accountants and financial consultants that rule business, unlike in the US, where the lawyers rule.

After university, I just felt grateful to be offered a position with a worldwide leader in business. However, did I really think about what I was doing? Not really! I just went along with the whole machine.

I often tell students, that it is beneficial to get trained by a major corporation early in your career. Learn what you need to learn and have those credentials on your resume. Then once you feel comfortable, leave and start your own company.

The environment to create your own business is so much more encouraging in the USA compared to England. The USA actively encourages people to start their own business.

I was trained in business by a major firm. I learnt the film business from a major firm. I consulted in media in Europe. When I saw a new technology emerging, namely home video, which was about to boom all over the world, I jumped at the chance to be part of it. I was European with excellent contacts in Europe; therefore, it made sense for me to take the plunge and open my own international home video business. (career #5)

Of course, owning your own business means you are responsible for everything including paying yourself. It's all you! For me that was scary. However, I was doing something I loved and knew that in that environment and at that stage of the video boom industry I had a great chance to be successful and happy.

"Success consists of going from failure to failure without loss of enthusiasm."
Winston Churchill

LEFT SIDE RIGHT SIDE
It is interesting to discuss whether you feel you are a left side of the brain person or a right side of the brain person? Are you the creative type or the numbers type? Business, finance or creative, marketing... Or both?

People tend to view themselves one dimensionally - artist or accountant.

In general, the left and right hemispheres of your brain process information in different ways. We tend to process information using our dominant side; however, the learning and thinking process is enhanced when both side of the brain participate in a balanced manner.

The two sides of the brain each have distinct capabilities and your strengths and weaknesses are frequently based upon the side of your brain that is dominant.

Are you right or left?
People who are left-brain thinkers are often better at and enjoy math and science over art and literature, making them perfect candidates for a career in engineering.

Socially-oriented people are usually right-brain thinkers. Right-brain thinkers love visual explanations over text explanations and are more interested in the initial creative process.

Those who are left-brain thinkers are more into processing information and analyzing the details than focusing on the creative. So which are you and does it affect your thoughts on a career path?

In my early career, I focused on math, accounting and finance. These skills would benefit me in business. Later, when I wanted to expand in to marketing, selling and distribution, I realized I had these additional creative skills! Both sides of my brain came into play.

I first tasted marketing and public relations at 20th Century Fox. But it was not until I had my own business that I found I had creative talents and had a flair for them. I was acquiring films, selling films, marketing and distributing films all over the world. Creating and *assessing marketing, sales campaigns for films worldwide. All new skills.*

Being trained in financial and business skills proved very beneficial; however, owning my own business also allowed me to utilize all the new creative and marketing skills I developed.

So the left brain, right brain concepts in my case complimented each other!

STEP 2: WHERE ARE YOU NOW
(PRESENT CAREER & LIFE)

EVALUATE YOUR SITUATION

The ability to focus and analyze where you are presently in your career is an important step in your evaluation of where you might wish to go. How can you decide where you wish to go, if you do not fully appreciate where you are at present?

Is it time for a serious re-evaluation of your career status? Is it potentially time to make changes? How do you know when you need to change your career path?

Are you ready to face that career change plunge? Do you wish you were? Take the time and make sure what you really want to do is change careers. There is no doubt that the employment climate in the decade starting at 2010 is very different than the last few decades. Boomers really must evaluate where they are now and make decisions based on many factors.

To help answer these questions a full and complete review is required to evaluate where you are now! Many people procrastinate and let things slide, as the thought of looking at their career is daunting. It is a positive step to even think of taking stock and looking where you are and in what state your career is in.

Many factors will go into a decision of such importance. It may be forced on you or it may be voluntary. The new career world order tells us that changing careers is the new norm, not the exception.

Remember that career change is a natural life progression. Most studies show that the average person working will change careers several times over the course of their lifetime. Notice we are distinguishing careers from job changes.

- ✓ Are you happy?
- ✓ Are you challenged?
- ✓ Are you compensated adequately?
- ✓ Do you have job satisfaction?
- ✓ Do you feel your career is going in the right direction?
- ✓ What are your priorities in life and your career?

Each stage of the Five Step Approach demands considerable effort, focus and determination to thoroughly evaluate who you are; what you truly want; what you need to do and what you need to have at your disposal to help you attain success.

To seriously look at your present career and all aspects of your career, is a task not to be taken lightly. To sit down and fully evaluate what, why and how you are doing in your present situation can be overwhelming. To clinically analyze how you arrived here and what your present situation holds for you in terms of satisfaction, happiness and fulfillment requires thought. A true assessment of your situation is required.

If you find you are not happy; you are not satisfied; you are not fulfilled, should this prompt you to make some fundamental decisions and the biggest one should be to ACT?

To do nothing simply perpetuates your present unsatisfactory situation.

RE-INVENT YOURSELF
The process of re-inventing yourself is very much an action orientated exercise that is very important to every person thinking of changing or adjusting careers. Your ability to examine yourself in a critical manner will benefit you as you move into action.

Understanding where you are at the present will give you a clear insight to where you need to go. Self-analysis is an important aspect of your journey. To be able to evaluate yourself critically and with honesty is integral part of the process.

> **Identify your strengths?**
> **Identify your weaknesses?**
> **What are potential opportunities?**
> **What threats are identified?**

By answering these questions honestly, you will gain clarity on your career choices. Whether to move into another role within your current situation; to leave; to move into a totally new area or even start your own company is your choice. This process is very important.

Step 2: Where Are You Now | 75

Strengths:
    Identify your strengths.
    What are your most marketable career skills?
    Which transferable skills are truly transferable?
    What are your leadership and managerial skills?
    Examine your educational and professional qualifications.

Weaknesses:
    What are your weaknesses?
    What areas require attention?
    Additional educational or professional qualifications?

Opportunities:
    New opportunities to be found?
    Identify new industries, new technologies.
    What is the level of demand for your skills and talents?

Threats:
    What are the potential negatives?
    Business or industry problems?

Look to my career path especially in the last ten years and you will see the very essence of re-inventing yourself!

"The most difficult thing in life is to know yourself"
                                                                    Thales

---

I started career #6 (university lecturer) in Seattle, then moved to Miami; however, family issues caused me to leave Miami. I returned to the Seattle area and set up house in a rural area some two hour drive from Seattle in a stunning part of the world, the Olympic Peninsula.

This move physically isolated me. I had earlier in my career commuted three days a week to Seattle to teach at the University of Washington as a part-time marketing adjunct professor. I was not prepared to continue such a tiring commute. Once again I had to re-evaluate what I really wanted to do in the circumstances I found myself in.

I had to look closely at my strengths and weaknesses at my present location:

My Strengths:
- ✓ *Very strong business experience*
- ✓ *Excellent university/college teaching credentials*
- ✓ *Held senior management positions in major companies*
- ✓ *Started and operated my own business for many years*
- ✓ *Considerable international business experience*
- ✓ *Most comfortable in project based activities*
- ✓ *Excellent teacher and public speaker*
- ✓ *Very knowledgeable in entertainment industry*
- ✓ *Excellent transferable skills*

My Weaknesses:
- ✓ *Located in rural area*
- ✓ *Two hour drive to nearest city*
- ✓ *Require more social media experience*
- ✓ *Getting older*

Based on my evaluation and my potential options, I decided teaching was no longer an option. I could not do the drive back and forth, two hours each way, every day.

After extensive thought and review, I came up with four areas of possible career avenues:

- ✓ *Seminars and webinars*
- ✓ *Book author*
- ✓ *Business consulting*
- ✓ *Film production/distribution*

Each activity did not require me to be in a major city. In fact, with a smartphone and internet, all these activities could be managed adequately and effectively. Each activity would require business trips to see clients at regular intervals, potentially all over the world. So far so good! Each of these activities would require me to utilize my extensive business experience gained in all my careers.

It would seem sensible to benefit and engage my vast experience in the entertainment industry, my excellent business credentials, my education achievements and my success in teaching and public speaking to create a new career.

My goal then became to create a seminar/webinar business based on my film industry experience; plus, any other activities that might fit the bill. To help provide further credibility in this venture I would write a book(s) about the film industry.

I also would need to create a business consulting practice, primarily in the entertainment sector, and other business areas I was familiar with.

Finally, I would continue on a reduced basis my film distribution and production business.

Career #7 (book author and seminar-webinar presenter) was born! My idea of having paying customers to attend a two day/one day seminar on a film industry topic was a great idea as it fulfilled all my requirements. Besides my many years in the film business, I also have strong teaching credentials at major universities. That provides immense credibility for my seminar-webinar proposal to the potential entertainment industry audience.

To add even more credibility I thought about writing a book about the independent film industry. Another new career was about to blossom, that of book author!

I, therefore, had three clearly defined tasks:

- ✓ *Prepare a career involving seminars on topics that would provide value to an audience*
- ✓ *Write books*
- ✓ *Identify the seminar audience and market to that audience*

The first two items I knew I could do them. It would take a great deal of work, but I really wanted to do them. It took about a year to write the book and get it published.

The book title is "The Film Biz Bible". I created a two day seminar around the book that incorporated the book contents. Great marketing idea I thought.

A more difficult task was to create a strategy on how to find and market to a potential seminar and book audience utilizing a limited budget. TV commercials were out and so was extensive advertising in major magazines – too much money.

The internet and social media were marketing tools. I had some knowledge of these areas. This created an opportunity to learn a new skill and a new industry. I needed to market myself using modern technology and the power of social media.

What a great skill to learn. It can only benefit me in the future. So for over a year, I studied and become very familiar with websites, social media and how to create internet marketing materials and target audiences using LinkedIn, Facebook, Meet ups and various community sites. Another new career was blossoming!

All these new ventures, I could actively work on from my remote rural setting. Hurray for modern technology and social media. A new self-employed career world was opening up for me.

NOTE: In the chapter, MY CAREER AFTER FIFTY, I describe in much more depth the journey I took and why I made certain decisions that lead me to career #6 and the three phases of career #7.

CAREER MYTHS
There are many myths about careers.

Money, money, money!
Money does not equal happiness. If you don't know that, then let me tell you right now it doesn't and countless surveys confirm that. Of course money is a prerequisite to live and you must decide what kind of living standard you wish to attain. Money is only one component of employment. So many people enjoy what they do at work and that is a much more important factor than money.

Career decisions are easy
No! To choose a career demands a great deal of thought and self-analysis and this will and can occur a number of times during your life. To define a career path, requires many steps and involves considerable time on self-evaluation and career research prior to decisions being taken.

Skills don't transfer
All skills are valuable. You have them naturally or you have learnt them and developed them over time. Certainly, new jobs may require those skills to be used in different ways. New skills might

Changing careers is impossible
Where there is a will there is a way. Research and discover new careers. There are so many ways to uncover new career paths.

Hobbies and careers don't mix
Many of our greatest minds and entrepreneurs have been very successful from developing careers from their hobbies and interests. When choosing a career, it makes perfect sense to fully evaluate a career that is related to a topic that you find interesting and enjoy.

> "That some achieve great success, is proof to all that others can achieve it as well."
> **Abraham Lincoln**

WHAT KIND OF PERSON ARE YOU
Look at yourself and decide what kind of person are you?

- A person who makes things happen
- A person who watches things happen
- A person who wonders what happened

Make an honest assessment of your skills, talents and traits. This is the first step on the journey to achieving your career goals.

> **"Accept responsibility for your life. Know that it is you who will get you where you want to go, no one else."**

We now anticipate changing careers will become even more prevalent due to the changes we are seeing in the employment environment of the 21st century.

> "In order to succeed, your desire for success should be greater than your fear of failure"
> **Bill Cosby**

WHAT IS SUCCESS

Success isn't what others can see, but how you feel. It's living your truth and doing what makes you truly happy.

> "Success is doing what you want, when you want, where you want, with whom you want, as much as you want"
> **Anthony Robbins**

Baby boomers, in most cases, have a good idea what success is! The question is more to do with how you feel personally about your own level of success and where that might lead you as you become a maturing baby boomer. Defining success rests with you and only you. Defining your goals helps you recognize, focus and act upon opportunities.

> "We learn wisdom from failure much more than success"
> **Samuel Smiles**

To make the decision to act means to do something about your situation; however, what to do and how to do it are very important questions that require thought and consideration.

> "Vision without action is daydream.
> Action without vision is nightmare"

MY CAREER AFTER FIFTY
(WHAT I DID AND HOW I DID IT!)

As I turned fifty, I realized that I was about to enter a whole new world. A new life, a new career!

- ✓ What career was I to follow?
- ✓ Would I have the required skills for my new career of choice?
- ✓ Would that career be viable where I chose to live (rural USA)?
- ✓ Could my new career provide sustainable income?

This book is a direct outcome of my search for answers to those questions. The journey of discovery I found myself taking was extremely revealing. I had to evaluate all my skills, wants, desires, personality and examine them in relation to the new employment environment. What I was going to do with the rest of my life? I was still very young at heart, physically fit, and full of experience and full of determination to be happy and fulfilled in whatever venture or ventures I was to discover.

I spent considerable time in researching and understanding social media both as a tool for potential employment prospects and also as a media that provides a wealth of self-employment and consulting business opportunities.

At this time of life (as a maturing boomer), it is certainly scary to realize that much of your old career is no longer viable and new paths need to be discovered.

I realized that what was happening to the employment market and the events of the financial crash, would cause my career path to be flexible and fluid. Nothing was secure and a constant state of career vigilance was necessary.

The days of secure job, secure career path were long gone. Being flexible; adapting to changing situations; making a full analysis of my skills and how to apply them and of course, the big one – learning new skills, especially in social media and internet were paramount.

The decade following my turning fifty has proven all of the above. Little did I know that I would find multiple new careers within that *period and totally embrace social media and the internet as avenues for potential business opportunities and self-employment.*

To help you follow my career path for the ten years since turning fifty years old, I have identified career #6 and career #7. Career #7 has three phases and continues today.

My first critical assessment led me to a university teaching career - Career #6 (My University Professor phase). Career #6 lasted six years and I taught at two universities (University of Miami and University of Washington).

My research involved detailed evaluation of many university websites and also connecting with LinkedIn and other internet sites that were specifically involved in adjunct professor employment.

Some of the questions that needed to be addressed were:

- ✓ *What was required in terms of educational credentials?*
- ✓ *What particular subject was I best suited for?*
- ✓ *University or colleges or both?*
- ✓ *Which type of university or college was available to me geographically?*
- ✓ *What about online teaching?*

My lecturing career proved to be incredibly rewarding. It gave me a great deal of personal satisfaction and pride. I felt proud that in some small way I helped students in their careers. However, that career had to come to an end as the extensive amount of commuting was becoming a major problem.

So as career #6 was fading, I needed to sit down and focus once again on my circumstances to come up with other viable career options.

I'm now well in to my fifties and I need another major re-evaluation!

So here comes career #7 with a few twists and turns!

Once again, I followed the Five Step Approach. Over the next four years I moved into a new career path. This path was based on the utilization of new technology and social media. However, I did fall back into my film industry mode one more time and ended up hitting a wall!

CAREER #7 *(Author/Seminar/Film/Social Media/ Speaker)*
  Location: Seattle, USA
  Company: My own media company
  Term: Four years to present
  Position: President

Career #7 comprises three phases:

PHASE #1: Film Seminars/Film Book Author
  Created personal brand "Mr. Film Biz" – marketed brand on Facebook; LinkedIn; Meetups etc.
  Created Mr. Film Biz website (www.mrfilmbiz.com)
  Created a two day "Film Business" seminar for paying customers.
  Wrote and published five books on the film business, including "The Film Biz Bible".

PHASE #2: Film Production: *Feature Film "Serenity Farm"*
  Produced and distributed a low budget thriller feature film (www.serenityfarmthemovie.com)

PHASE #3: Speaker/Changing Careers/Author/Social Media
  Wrote and published motivational book, Five Step Approach for baby boomers changing careers – "Change Your Career... Baby Boomers!"
  Created personal brand as speaker for Changing Careers... Baby Boomers
  Created website to market speaker engagements
  Extensive research on social media for marketing ventures
  Expanded into business entrepreneurial ventures
  (Faith based products - www.popesainthood.com)

Career #7 is still morphing today! Career #7 happened because of the voluntary ending of my university teaching career. I loved teaching at the universities; but, commuting was becoming too much.

Teaching provided confirmation of certain skills I thought I had, but had never tested. I found out I was an excellent communicator, good teacher, motivator with exceptional skills as a presenter and deliverer of ideas and situations.

Combining my extensive business experience and my newly confirmed skills as an educator and teacher, new opportunities would open up. Add to that mix a strong desire to understand social media, internet and new delivery technology, more avenues will become available.

Let's discuss in more detail the different career #7 phases.

PHASE #1: Film Seminars / Film Book Author

The idea of being able to host a two day seminar on certain aspects of the film industry and charge a fee for attendance was an appealing business model. After all, there are film people all over the world and the idea of presenting a film seminar was exciting to me.

A marketing vehicle and a strong social media presence was required to help market the seminars to targeted audiences. Also, I decided that I should write a book on the film business. This would help enhance my stature in the film community and would provide additional revenue from book sales.

The business model was set:

- ✓ Create a social media presence by creating a film industry/social media persona. That is how "Mr. Film Biz" was born! We actively pursued creating a social media presence as "Mr. Film Biz" on Facebook, Twitter and on the film industry websites, pages and meetups etc. – A strong expanse of social media connections.
- ✓ As part of my seminar credentials, I wrote and published a book on the film business "The Film Biz Bible".
- ✓ A creative and highly functional "Mr. Film Biz" website was produced with numerous blogs, video clips, etc.
- ✓ A full two day seminar was created and presented on the website and actively projected into social media.
- ✓ Various targeted geographical areas were selected for dates of the seminars and marketing campaigns were set to focus on maximizing attendance at set seminars.

If this business model would work it could be very lucrative and fun.

PHASE #2: Film Production – Feature Film "Serenity Farm"

As I was creating the seminar and writing the book, "The Film Biz Bible", I came up with the idea of shooting a feature film in the location I was living. I would also write about the experience in my film book. It would add great content for my seminar.

I would sell the film and make money... what a great idea!

Well it didn't exactly go as planned. I produced a really good thriller film (www.serenityfarmthemovie.com); however, since the film has been finished I have had lots of trouble selling it to all the different media, both in the USA and foreign, for any significant money.

How could this happen? After all, I have produced and sold many films in my film career. Well guess what?... the market and the technology passed me bye and the demand for these kind of low budget, no name films, had over the last few years dropped dramatically. Therefore, selling the film has proved to be a big disappointment. I'm still working on getting sales but it's not easy! I hit a wall!

Looking on the bright side, It provided a great deal of material for my film seminars and an informative chapter in my book.

The first two phases of career #7 were moving along nicely. My desire to expand my career horizons was still strong. My focus on continuing with my seminars and even expanding to webinars was clear. How could I expand my career potential?

As time passed, I discussed what was happening in my career path with a number of my close friends and I realized my journey was an inspiration to them. They urged me to write about my journey. Be motivational and even inspirational to other people in similar situations.

I sat down and carefully thought about writing a book on career change and how I had approached my own journey during these years. I wanted the book to be helpful and provide a guide to others in a journey that is often overwhelming.

PHASE #3: Speaker; Author; Social Media; Consultant
I envisioned combining a book, website, speaking tours etc.; an all-in-one business venture, similar to my Mr. Film Biz persona business. This venture made sense to me! I could help baby boomers and other people, who are facing the apprehensive task of career change. Write a career motivational book; set up a website, and

most of all, speak to people about my experiences. Provide tools, techniques and strategies along the lines of my FIVE STEP CAREER CHANGING program. My desire to help others was strong.

As a baby boomer myself, I wanted to focus attention on boomers and convey to them how I followed the Five Step Approach to successfully change my career. At the same time I wanted my book and seminars to be relevant to any person in the same situation; young or old; male or female; richer or poorer; well-educated or not.

My new updated business model was set:

- ✓ Write and publish a motivational Five Step Approach book focused on baby boomers about changing careers – "Change Your Career... Baby Boomers!
- ✓ Create personal brand as speaker for Changing Careers …. Baby Boomers
- ✓ Utilize social media to market the book and speaker engagements
- ✓ Create website to market speaker, DVD, seminar and book (www.johnrodsett.com)

In addition, I wanted to expand my knowledge of social media and business marketing and selling in new media to help uncover more new business ventures... a process I am still very active in.

So you are now fully up to date on the life, the times and the career of John Rodsett!

"Success is a Choice"
Rick Pitino

STEP 3: WHAT YOU NEED TO HAVE
(STRATEGIES, TOOLS, SKILLS, TECHNIQUES)

Do you have the right tools, strategies, skills and techniques to succeed in your venture? You have skills and experience. They need to be identified, quantified and evaluated.

DO YOU HAVE WHAT IT TAKES
Which skills are best suited to achieving your goals? Without being specific to certain career paths we can identify certain skills that are required to be successful in any career.

Critical thinking
To be successful in business, critical thinking skills are important. To be able to process, evaluate and analyze data in an efficient manner and arrive at decisions based on your findings is a tremendous asset.

Decision making
The ability to evaluate a situation and make a clear focused decision based on information in a timely manner is a valuable skill. The lack of decision making capability can be a major flaw. A decision is a choice between two or more alternatives. They are a constant necessity and have to be made continuously in any business. Not making a decision is a decision. Decision making is an integral part of leadership.

When making decisions ensure you follow simple guidelines:

- ✓ Clearly understand the situation requiring attention
- ✓ Evaluate what caused the issue
- ✓ Analyze potential solutions to resolve the issue
- ✓ Make an informed decision
- ✓ Create a plan of action to solve the issue
- ✓ Review the effectiveness of your decision
- ✓ Ensure the issue is solved, if not re-evaluate

Good decision making requires attention and thought covering all aspects of the situation.

Listening

Many people talk about listening but rarely pay full attention. Learn the art of conversation and listening. Learn to study a person and pick up any and all body language and expressions or interests they show. Have a conversation that allows them to provide information about themselves, not just business. Try to connect and engage on a personal level as well as a business level.

We think we listen but we don't! We tend to see things the way we think they are, instead of how they really are. Listening is an important element in your professional career as is your ability to connect with other professionals.

Research indicates that seventy-five percent of the time we are preoccupied or distracted during conversations. We recall fifty percent of what we hear. Over a longer period, we remember only twenty percent of what we heard.

> "We only hear half of what is said to us,
> understand only half of that,
> believe only half of that and
> remember only half of that."

Most people will not pay attention to your point of view until they are reasonably assured you have heard and understood their point of view. It is so important to ensure you are communicating and listening effectively.

People skills

In my experience, this area is critical, yet so little time is provided in education or training to helping people understand people skills.

Your skills and abilities are very important; but, so are your relationships with colleagues, employees and business associates. Your ability to function in a positive and productive way with other people, is critical.

Part of your own self-evaluation is to be self-critical in evaluating how you are perceived at work. It is essential that you maintain a positive and respectful position in your work environment.

Always be professional and polite. Ensure you stay away from gossip, romance or negative comments. Positive emotions and high energy is a benefit. Negative emotions often create adverse reactions. How you interact with associates can mean the difference for success or failure.

One of the best bits of advice I was given at a young age was to evaluate each and every person who you work with. Identify their traits, interests and especially what motivates them. Take personal interest in everyone in a positive manner.

Do they teach work place relationship skills at university? They should! This is truly a minefield that can destroy your career. However, if you are good at it then it can be a great help. Which are you?

I will share with you a big mistake I made early in my career. I criticized my boss to a fellow colleague. That person told my boss. The backlash was immediate and unpleasant.

So please always be careful on being critical about anyone at work. It may come back to bite you.

Information assimilation
To gather large amounts of information from all sources and extrapolate and analyze data is another beneficial business skill.

Communication
Communication skills (both written and verbal) are high priorities. Whether you are climbing the management ladder or dealing with associates, your ability to communicate your decisions, points of view and needs in a clear, precise manner becomes even more essential.

Speaking
Your ability to be a good speaker is a business requirement. To present ideas verbally to audiences of all types and sizes, as well as easily change presentation styles, so as to meet an audience's demographics, is an highly effective skill. Whether it is, speaking to a small group about a project or a large room full of executives, the ability to speak clearly, articulately and with focus, is a career asset.

Fear of speaking in public is often a reality. There are many courses and instructional approaches available to help reduce levels of anxiety. Here are a few tips that have helped me overcome my fear of public speaking:

- ✓ Talk about something you really know and understand
- ✓ Be excited about your topic
- ✓ Engage your audience
- ✓ Talk from the heart
- ✓ Be positive and engaging
- ✓ Talk about your personal experiences
- ✓ Make it simple - Be simple
- ✓ Make brief card notes – never write out your talk
- ✓ Have illustrations and examples
- ✓ Rehearse
- ✓ Work on delivery
- ✓ Do not be boring
- ✓ Humor is good
- ✓ Be yourself
- ✓ Know when to stop

I was always extremely nervous about speaking in public. I remember at 20th Century Fox having to speak to a number of USC students and being physically sick before the talk. I also remember going to see a hypnotist to try and help me overcome my fear of public speaking.

Over time I focused on many of the points I listed above. I gained confidence in my ability to speak in public to the point I now really enjoy it. I still get nervous; but, I view that as a positive to ensure I focus and do well.

Motivation
To motivate yourself and others is part of being a leader. To evaluate and determine other people's motivation and apply your communication skills to create an environment of clear goals and tasks is of great benefit.

Delegating
The desire to pass on the authority and responsibility to another person to carry out specific activities is delegation. Your ability to

effectively delegate will ensure goals and tasks are completed in an efficient and timely manner.

Networking
Networking is a vital aspect of your career success. It requires substantial time to develop a full understanding of the various tools and requirements available to enhance your networking capabilities. Networking is discussed in more detail in Step 5.

Initiative
Take the initiative, but do so professionally. Use your skills to initiate action and get things done efficiently and effectively.

Prioritization
To prioritize, means to list tasks or goals in some order that focuses attention on what has to be done and in what order. They must be developed in a disciplined and focused manner. We need to identify tasks that are to be accomplished, identify the level of importance of each task and the associated effort required. Once this is done, evaluate all tasks and make a judgment on a priority list.

Perseverance
To persevere means you need to eliminate obstacles, stay on course and not give up. Persist and move forward with your tasks unless you are certain a change is needed.

"Don't worry about failures, worry about the chances you miss when you don't even try."
Jack Canfield

ACTIVITY v's ACCOMPLISHMENT
Do not confuse activity with accomplishment. Working hard does not necessarily mean working efficiently or effectively. Activity does not necessarily equate with being productive.

Does anyone have all these business skills? The more you do have the better. Many of us have a number of these skills in various levels of competency, but few have all those skills at the highest levels of proficiency.

As your career develops, your own strengths and weaknesses will become more apparent. Be truthful in your career evaluation and identify those areas that require attention. In my own personal evaluation, I noticed as I became more experienced in the work place, I learnt many lessons "on the job".

One particular business skill I have paid close attention to concerns the ability to understand what makes the other person tick! What are their motivations? What are their true wants and needs? Try to understand what interests them and what lights them up. If you understand their motivation, it allows you to get on to their wave length easier; and, hopefully makes business go more smoothly.

Another skill I found valuable for my career path was the ability to focus on what's important - not only on the big picture items, but also on the smaller tasks. I certainly learnt that skill in real time at the Los Angeles Summer Olympic Games.

The LAOOC was a one billion dollar start-up company (The Los Angeles Olympic Organizing Committee) that had to be fully operational in less than eighteen months. Once the Olympic Games event was completed the whole organization would be closed down in six months.

For the two years I was working at the Organizing Committee as VP Controller, it was one huge series of critical tasks that had to be given priorities and completed on time. Opening Ceremonies for the Summer Olympics was set in stone - a world-wide audience was set to turn on their TV's at opening ceremonies - everything had to be in place and working. Everyone had clear and defined tasks and goals that had to be accomplished – no excuses!

The Olympic Games (career #3) was the ultimate in motivation and a serious challenge. You had to accomplish your goals otherwise billions of people around the world would see an empty TV screen and no Olympic Games! Failure was not an option. If you couldn't do the job you were fired and someone else brought in.

The most intense, challenging job ever.

Your ability to think on your feet, to have critical thinking skills was paramount at the Olympics. Decisions had to be made quickly and made on information available at the time. Time was critical. What's more, you had no one to go to for advice on how to do your job because no one had done an Olympics the way we were doing it.

We worked twenty-four hours a day, seven days a week, for two years, to build the organization that was the $1 billion Summer Olympic Games.

Luckily for us, it became the most amazing Olympics and the most financially successful ever. The Los Angeles Olympic Games business model became the blueprint for many future worldwide events.

"Enter every activity without giving mental recognition to the possibility of defeat. Concentrate on your strengths, instead of your weaknesses… on your powers, instead of your problems"
                                                                    Paul J. Meyer

---

WHAT DOES EDUCATION MEAN
The days of obtaining education without a clear aim and focus for a career path appear to have vanished. A student should have a strong sense of what their degree can contribute in terms of a future career.

It is unreasonable to assume a student at eighteen years old, knows what career they will follow. However, in today's competitive world with the high cost of education, it seems there is a necessity to choose a degree and choose a career that can work in harmony for your future.

In the USA, many people are educated to a degree standard. In England access to universities is more restricted and entry requirements are very high; therefore, the percentage of the population with degrees is much less than in the US.

Having so many people with degrees in the US means competition is strong. Not having a degree may hamper your career prospects. One of the great benefits of the US degree system is that you can gain access to the programs at any age and for any discipline. All you need are the right grades and credits, plus the money or the loans to pay for it.

Do you need higher education?
Education is a basic requirement. Obtaining a college type education has been the traditional way; however, are other avenues available for career advancement?

The employment career paradigm has changed. Has the education needs of our new world moved with the times? In general it is true that the more you educate yourself, the more opportunities will be open.

In today's competitive employment market, employers put a higher value on college degrees. Statistics show that college graduates, in general, have far more successful careers and earn more money over the course of their working life, than do non-graduates. For many professions, a higher degree is required. Education credentials help ensure you have the right training and expertise.

What kind of education do you need depends on two things:

> What sort of career you want?
> How long you are prepared to go to school?

With a only a high school education employment opportunities are limited. With a technical institute diploma you can certainly focus on the skilled trades (i.e. electricians, welder, fabricators etc.). University degrees, especially in courses in demand, open up a wide array of career potential both in management and technical fields.

Skills, not just education?
As a point of discussion, it can be said that the unemployed do not need more school, they need more skills.

Employers need people with specific abilities. Degrees and diplomas are credentials. They do not, by themselves, guarantee that the person possesses the skills an employer requires. However, does the education system provide that service? When your skills and abilities match a position, then we have a match. Your skill set is the key to opportunities.

People with college degrees are generally able to find jobs of some kind. The unemployment level for college graduates is about half that of high school graduates and almost three times better than for those with no high school diploma. Education should help you provide the skills industry requires.

The choice of degree and the type of career should complement each other.

Choosing new career paths is not easy. The career of a university lecturer (career #6) appealed and demanded certain educational requirements.

My excellent education was from an English university, not from a US university. Also, part of my post-graduate education was a professional accounting and finance based qualification that would not necessarily be fully accredited in the USA. To meet the educational requirements required for a university adjunct professor position, I needed to enhance my educational standards. I decided to obtain a Master of Science degree.

This took time, effort and money. Without this post-graduate degree, I might not have been accredited by the university and could not have qualified for the lecturer faculty position. In my case, further education was needed and it was for a specific purpose. It would enable me to meet the requirements of a specific job in a specific industry.

> "There is no better education like adversity"
> Benjamin Disraeli

YOU NEED CAREER MANAGMENT
Career management means taking an active involvement in where your career is going. This demands thought and contemplation. The outcome of successful career management should ensure professional fulfillment, a balanced life and career, effective goal achievement and financial security. Taking your career into your own hands, molding it to what you wish and finding the career plan that works for you. That is career management.

Focus on career opportunities that are practical, realistic and attainable. Always be aware of what type of career goal you are aiming for and what qualifications are required. Your success, your opportunities are a function of your planning, evaluation and the career roadmap you have created. The methods you use to conduct your search; the contacts in your network; the number of opportunities available in your area; your desire to work hard in your pursuit to find that right career are part of your strategy to succeed.

Choose your industry carefully. Once you choose your target industry, make sure to tailor your resume accordingly. Even if you don't have experience directly related to your new career, you have transferable skills from previous work. Present your skills, experience and abilities clearly. They are your passport to a new career. Be determined to convey your commitment to ensure your skills are current and remain up-to-date with the latest technical advances in your field. Your drive to perform and maintain high standards is critical.

It can be said that a person is always in career management mode, focusing on new potential opportunities and maintaining your status as a viable candidate. There is a need to look to the future and focus on maintaining skills; building up networks; researching industries and be attentive to new developments. Career management demands thought and should include all aspects of your goals, experience and skills.

By definition career management means managing your career. In many cases people do not manage their career. They often leave it up to fate and random events, often beyond their own control. They react rather than plan.

During the early stages of my work life I was guided by what my peers at university were doing. The best students got recruited by a top accounting firm, got a great salary, moved to London and got great professional training (career #1). After four years, you obtained the professional qualification, then went out into industry or stayed in the accounting tax profession. In this scenario I found myself very unhappy in my professional accounting career path. It was not my cup of tea at all!

I needed so much more. I decided drastic action was needed. I made the decision to leave England and go to the USA to find new opportunities. That was a drastic course of action, especially as I had no idea how this whole journey was going to work out.

Pretty scary career management! That drastic course of action changed my life for the better. (Careers #2, 3, 4 and 5)

I was employed by 20th Century Fox in Los Angeles in the finance and production areas. Soon I decided to actively pursue a move into marketing and distribution. At the time, Fox Studios had produced "Star Wars", so I saw firsthand the marketing genius of product marketing and merchandising on a grand scale. I actively embraced tasks in marketing and distribution, both in TV and feature films. Years later, the marketing and distribution experience I had gained at Fox benefited me greatly in my own company.

Another example of my own career management was career #6, university lecturer.

Earlier in my book I described at some length the processes I went through to follow my goal of becoming a university adjunct professor/lecturer. That reality began at the University of Washington. (career #6)

My university lecturer path developed further when I decided I wanted to manage this new teaching career by re-locating from the Seattle area to Miami, Florida. In so doing, I was making another important career management decision.

Prior to living in the Seattle area, I lived in sunny Los Angeles for many years. I missed the sunny warm weather. South Florida beckoned; and, in particular, Miami. I needed to research and find a university that fit my requirements for a position as a university adjunct professor in marketing or in film. (career #6 – but in different location)

I researched extensively a number of educational establishments in Florida. I sent numerous cover letters, plus resumes, to heads of departments in my selected area of expertise. The letters highlighted my business background, my educational qualifications and my recent successful teaching period at the University of Washington.

During my research the University of Miami was prominent. I noticed their website referred to only PhD lecturers should apply for lecturer positions. This was initially disappointing, but I persevered and sent a letter to the Chair of the Marketing Dept. at the School of Business Administration at the University of Miami. My letter mentioned I would be visiting Miami on a certain date and it would be a pleasure to meet him.

Surprise, surprise, I received a note back to please come and see him at a certain time and date. I thought that was a positive; however, I thought my chances of getting a position would be slim, due to the PhD requirement.

Suffice to say, I went into the University in Miami. The university was absolutely stunning – beautiful grounds, lovely buildings and of course great weather. I met the department head and had a great meeting with him. At the end of the meeting he offered me a part-time position for the next semester. I could not believe it! I was being offered a position as adjunct professor teaching International Marketing at the University of Miami, School of Business.

As the old saying goes "nothing ventured, nothing gained". I had rolled the dice and struck gold!

I ended up working at the University of Miami for two fabulous years. During that time, I was promoted to a full-time lecturer, plus I also taught Motion Picture Marketing at the School of Communication at UM.

My two favorite subjects at a really amazing university. Lucky me! How was that for career management?

> "There are two primary choices in life: to accept conditions as they exist or accept the responsibility for changing them"
> **Denis Waitley**

YOU NEED TIME MANAGEMENT
Time management is planning and exercising control over the amount of time spent on specific activities in order to increase effectiveness, efficiency or productivity.

Time management is a skill. You need practice and you need discipline. Organization allows you to plan. If you plan you can prioritize. To assess how much time each of the tasks and goals will take is another skill. Such skills will allow you the ability to effectively manage your time against a planned agenda.

Some useful time management tips:

- ✓ Be specific and define your tasks
- ✓ Prioritize your tasks
- ✓ Focus and maintain your discipline
- ✓ Be consistent
- ✓ Have a routine

"Don't say you don't have enough time. You have exactly the same number of hours per day that were given to Michelangelo, Leonardo da Vinci, Thomas Jefferson, and Albert Einstein"

H. Jackson Brown Jr.

WORK HARD, WORK SMART

Working hard is an essential quality. What does working hard really mean? Sitting at a desk for hours does not mean you are working hard or being productive.

Productive and efficient work is the goal. Working hard is only one component of being successful. Working hard does not guarantee success. Think before you begin work and ensure you are approaching your tasks with due care and thought. The aim is to complete each task as quickly and effectively as possible.

To work smart means focus on being highly effective and efficient.

I like to think I can work hard and work smart. Whenever a task needs to be completed, I always try and evaluate how best to attack the problem. Tasks can be accomplished in many ways and it is up to you to figure out the most efficient and effective ways to do that.

Use your experience and knowledge to evaluate a task. Ultimately, hard work will be needed to complete the task.

*I remember vividly at the Los Angeles Olympic Games (**career #3**) one of my tasks was to build from scratch, a financial control system for the Olympic Games.*

We had twenty-two sports, many venues, a large organization and a one billion dollar budget that had to start up quickly and close down – all within two years!

As if that was not enough, the financial control system had to be able to completely switch from a horizontal based financial system to a vertical system a few months before the Games started.

Let me explain further! During the initial set-up of the accounting and financial systems of the Games, all systems were horizontally based. Meaning all costs were centrally controlled by centrally based departments (personnel, construction, transportation etc.) at the Olympic Headquarters.

A few months before the Games were to begin, this large financial control system was to be flipped and placed in to a vertical control mode. This meant the whole financial and accounting control system was to be sport venue based, not central headquarters based. We had to switch our financial and control systems to twenty-two different venues controlled at each of the twenty-two physical sites of the individual sports.

Not only did we work hard, but we had to work smart because we truly had a fixed timeline and no one had ever done such a feat! I am glad to report the task was accomplished without a hitch!

"The surest way not to fail is to determine to succeed"
Richard Brinsley Sheridan

DO YOU NEED TO BE PERFECT
Perfect is a word I try never to use. Perfection and excellence are not the same thing! It is not necessarily the case that perfectionism is the pursuit of excellence.

Perfection is an attitude that cannot be fully attained, therefore, why would you wish to feel you need to do more and feel that you are falling short. Be careful that the concept of perfection can lead you down a path of disappointment.

The pursuit of excellence and doing a great job are what we should aspire to. Perfection is unobtainable so why bother!

> "Be humble enough to admit you're not perfect,
> but determined enough to strive to be perfect"
> **Babsie Burk**

WE ALL HAVE TRANSFERABLE SKILLS
Transferable skills are the skills acquired during your working career. These skills are an integral part of the baby boomers pool of assets. The concept of transferable skills is a vital career component.

Unlike job-related skills, which tend to be used only in one type of employment, transferable skills are skills that can be used in every occupation, regardless of the type of work. They are universal skills — you can transfer them from one type of work to another without much effort on your part or training from the employer.

Transferable skills can be listed under these segments:

> **Management:** Supervise assignments and complete tasks
> **Communication**: Connect, create and direct information
> **Human Resource:** People and inter-personal skills
> **Operational:** Scheduling and efficiency skills
> **Problem Solving:** Analytical and decision making skills

These transferable skill sets are all part of your personal career asset portfolio.

> "A real decision is measured by the fact that you've taken action.
> If there's no action, you haven't truly decided."
> **Tony Robbins**

Your career roadmap requires that your transferable skills should be identified and analyzed:

First, identify your transferable skills
It's important to review in depth, each job you've held in order to discover what skills you actually have.

Second, do your skills fit your future career path?
Self-assessment is essential to helping find your career path. Part of this should involve finding out what careers best utilize your skills.

Finally, clearly present your transferable skills
Once all your transferable skills are identified, those skills must be presented in a clear and concise manner.

Education helps train your mind and provide a certain level of skill especially at the university degree level. Higher education trains you to think critically, examine problems, find solutions and then put those solutions into action. Higher education teaches you how to work in groups and analyze problems in a group.

Once you are employed, those skills are enhanced and true work place experiences contribute to those skills.

I must be a poster child for transferable skills! Over the years I gained proficiency in many of the transferable skills listed.

I realized early in my career that my personality suited project based assignments. Projects have a start, middle and end. Once completed you move on to another project. I like the challenge of new things. I like to know it will end. I like to complete a task then on to the next one. I don't like being bored!

In London, all my jobs were project based. In the US, at 20th Century Fox (career #2) everything was project based. Each film or TV series was a project.

My own media company (career #5) had lots of film projects that needed to be produced, distributed, marketed and sold. Once again it was project based.

Teaching at university (career #6) was project driven. You teach a set course or courses, to a set number of students, who take the course then leave. Later, a new set of students come in – a new project begins.

One of the reasons why the Olympics Game Organizing Committee (career #3) came to me at 20th Century Fox, was the fact they knew I was project orientated and had experience of handling major projects worth many millions of dollars – starting them, running them, then closing them out. My skill set was ideal for the Summer Games.

During my process of changing careers, I had to identify those skills and find careers that would suite them. I know I'm happiest in project management. My skills are best suited for that work environment.

Go where your strengths and passions are and those decisions will probably make you the happiest.

"Success is a state of mind. If you want success, start thinking of yourself as a success"
Dr. Joyce Brothers

STEP 4: HOW TO GET THERE
(PLAN OF ACTION / CAREER ROADMAP)

We have progressed through Steps 1, 2 and 3. These steps have created the platform to focus on Stage 4... Career Roadmap! By this stage, a pathway has been created to provide a vehicle, a template to achieve success.

Once you have created your plan of action, you will need to execute. It's all about creating the roadmap based on the goals you have so diligently developed and adopted for your career.

WHAT IS A CAREER ROADMAP
To be successful you need a plan – a career roadmap to help guide you and keep you on the right path. A career roadmap will help you create a clear set of tasks and goals that are uniquely your career DNA. The roadmap will assist you in creating a well-defined action plan to provide you the focus and confidence necessary to attain those goals.

A general broad stroke approach to goal setting is:

- ✓ Define the major goals for your new career
- ✓ Major goals comprise of many smaller manageable goals
- ✓ Create a plan of action – a career roadmap
- ✓ Implement the career roadmap
- ✓ Review regularly and make adjustments

Stage by stage goal setting
The first stage in setting goals is to consider what you want to achieve in your career, your life, in the long-term. Long-term may mean five or ten years – your decision. Setting these major goals provides the overall template that shapes all other aspects of your decision making.

Various aspects requiring your attention include but not limited to:

Location – Where do you wish to live?
Career – What are your career aspirations?
Education – What levels of education will be needed?
Financial – What financial resources are required?
Family – How do you balance family with career?

Values – What are your values, your principles?
Health – Personal health is important.
Leisure – What value do you place on leisure time?

Goals need to be stated and priorities set based on your personal preferences and desires. Once the major goals are identified and documented, these goals need to be broken down into manageable smaller tasks. Each major goal is a culmination of many smaller tasks. Each task must be completed in order for the larger goal to be achieved.

These smaller goals will be definite, manageable and time sensitive. Often short-term goals can be anywhere from months to a couple of years. Within each of these smaller tasks there will be identified even smaller tasks, with even shorter completion time periods.

The pyramid of goal success is set. From small tasks the larger goals are met and as each small task is completed, your level of confidence and success rises. Keep in mind that as your plan unfolds, there may be a need for revisions and adjustments.

This stage by stage approach for goal setting, from your initial long-term goals; to shorter more manageable goals; to virtually tiny daily tasks, will ensure your career roadmap will be detailed and fully functional. It will provide the blueprint necessary to help you meet your career goals.

Goal setting approach in summary:

What do you really want to do?
This big question needs to be answered.

Career goals must be identified
Focus on career objectives.
Self-evaluation and assessment is required.

Set your career goals and tasks
Identify and clarify your career goals in detail.
Set meaningful and attainable goals.
Every task has a clearly defined outcome and time frame.
Each task is a building block in achieving your larger goal.

Pay attention to the resources needed. Resources will include; but, are not limited to education, financial resources, time and effort, new and present skills, review of your abilities and support of family and friends.

Create a career roadmap
Your goals are identified. Activities and resources you require are listed. Once in action, regular review and adjustment is needed.

Call for action
The roadmap needs to be executed. Daily, weekly, monthly and annual calls for action are required.

"In absence of clearly defined goals, we become strangely loyal to performing daily acts of trivia"
Claude M. Bristol

WHAT ELSE IS REQUIRED AS PART OF YOUR CAREER ROADMAP
In addition to the goal setting process, there are a number of other aspects that require attention and focus:

Networking
In today's world, networking has grown in importance. Your ability to network can enhance your business stature significantly.

Personal and social media networking and the contacts generated are a vital aspect of any career roadmap:

> **Personal Contacts**
> **LinkedIn:** Personal connects and groups
> **Facebook:** Personal/groups
> **Twitter**
> **Meetup groups:** Your industry/job type
> **Internet communities:** Your industry/job type
> **Websites:** Career resources
> **Career websites:** Detailed assistance/resume etc.
> **Industry websites**
> **Job websites**

Your networking has to be effective, concentrated and time effective. The avenues available today to network are vast. Learn about them and how to use them.

Mentor
Changing careers is a major life decision that can get overwhelming. Find a mentor with knowledge of your future career path or career change expertize. A mentor can help in providing advice and guidance.

Flexible
Many things will move and change during this process. Being flexible, being able to move and re-direct based on changing circumstances is required.

Organized, persistent, consistent
It is so important to maintain a positive energy and focus. Daily, weekly, monthly organized tasks will ensure a consistent work approach. Effort, hard work and focus are required.

Personal brand
Create your personal marketing brand. This is so important and time consuming, but very necessary. Explained in more detail in Step 5.

WHAT DOES A CAREER ROADMAP LOOK LIKE
Every individual will have their own way of developing and creating their career roadmap.

We all are unique in our career skills, experiences and education. We also have our own career desires and goals. Therefore, no two career roadmaps will be the same.

The following is a broad stroke outline of my own career roadmap.

I created this roadmap at the age of fifty, after my career path and life changed significantly. It is important to understand that a career roadmap is a functional guide to assist you in focusing and accomplishing your goals. Over the last ten years, my career roadmap has changed and morphed. I followed each of the steps in my book and that enabled me to construct an effective and practical roadmap.

Step 4: How To Get There | 109

MY CAREER GOALS:
These are my goals based on past work experience; self-analysis; strengths and weaknesses; my wants and desires plus answers to the questions...

What do I want to do?
Where do I want live?
How do I earn money?

- ✓ Be self-employed
- ✓ Develop a business that can operate anywhere in the world
- ✓ Desire to inspire and infuse people and help contribute to their success
- ✓ Be happy!
- ✓ Focus on projects and international marketing based products
- ✓ Earn enough money to live comfortably
- ✓ Become a public speaker and presenter
- ✓ Identify my areas of expertise – entertainment, marketing, global business
- ✓ Become a university lecturer
- ✓ Become a book author
- ✓ Present seminars around the world in my areas of expertise
- ✓ Business consulting in my areas of expertise
- ✓ Be an entrepreneur when opportunity arises
- ✓ Film producing and media distribution in conjunction with books and seminars
- ✓ My location was to be rural – nowhere near a big city

WHAT I NEEDED TO DO TO ATTAIN THOSE GOALS:

- ✓ Fully evaluate my skills and business strengths and weaknesses
- ✓ Develop a schedule of short-term goals and longer-term goals within my total goal strategy
- ✓ Obtain graduate degree for university lecturing credentials
- ✓ Ensure my foreign education credits were acceptable for university lecturer applications
- ✓ Research universities and courses that were in my areas of expertise
- ✓ Prepare resume and cover letter for university departments that fit my skills

- ✓ Highlight my extensive business experience with major companies and international organizations especially in the field of marketing and global business
- ✓ Book author - what subjects, how to get published and how will these books assist me in my career goals?
- ✓ Seminars – what subjects, what kind of seminars and where and how to present?
- ✓ Understand and create major social media presence to market my personal brand
- ✓ Personal career branding on social media and website design for each area of my expertise - media and entertainment; film producing and distribution; seminars and books; business consulting; business entrepreneur
- ✓ Understand and apply website design techniques
- ✓ Understand and apply book publishing
- ✓ Understand and apply all forms of social media and personal branding
- ✓ Find mentors in the seminar, university teaching and book publishing areas

TIME PERIOD
Long-term was five years with multiple goals set medium-term and many short-term goals

---

**"Losers visualize the penalties of failure.
Winners visualize the rewards of success"**
William S. Gilbert

STEP 5: WHAT YOU NEED TO DO
(ACTION / EXECUTE)

This step is all about execution!

Once the career roadmap has been created, action is required. The career roadmap provides a comprehensive list of goals and tasks that need to be completed on a daily, weekly, monthly or annually basis.

Career plans are only as good as the ability of the person to act and execute the tasks required. The ability to execute and follow the roadmap in a timely fashion is important to your success.

The film "Field of Dreams" provided an interesting quote - "If you build it... They will come". In marketing your talents they need to know you exist and are worth the trip! Marketing yourself is a key ingredient of your career asset portfolio.

Certain aspects of your career roadmap are extremely important and require additional discussion.

PERSONAL CAREER BRAND
Personal self-branding has become extremely important in the career marketplace. An online personal branding strategy needs to be created, managed and put into action. Personal career branding is about defining who you are; your attributes; your goals. It is about identifying what makes you unique and how you can contribute and create value to future clients and companies.

Your profile must clearly identify your accomplishments; highlight your strengths and skills; list your education; state your professional qualifications; identify your work experience and any other attributes that can provide and create a level of quality differentiation from your competitors.

The profile should stand out and be highly presentable and professional. Your personal career brand reflects who and what you are in the business community. Your marketing has to be effective and consistent.

Promote your career brand in every source and avenue available. That includes, but is not limited to - all platforms of social media; publications and magazines; articles; blogs; networking groups; websites, and of course, LinkedIn and Facebook.

Your personal brand needs to be established and marketed just like any other brand in business - except it is "YOU". It is you marketing "you", as part of your career change strategy.

Do not underestimate the time, thought and preparation it takes to complete and maintain this very important task. Creating profiles for all the various online sites and making sure you maximize your potential is very important. Research social media sites and compare your profile with others that you may be competing with.

Marketing yourself is all about the need to create, revise, polish, and publish your own career brand. Marketing will enhance your exposure to opportunities. Create a profile that will attract and impress clients and businesses.

Ensure that your social media branding targets the businesses, industries and people that will benefit you in your future career choice. In my case, I had to re-define many of my skills and attributes focused on a new venture; therefore, my brand statement was very different from my past careers. This took time and research to create my brand suitable for my new career focus.

Self-promotion or marketing of "YOU" sounds self-indulgent and overwhelming. However, the ability to market yourself is much easier than years ago and is an important element of your career development. It takes time to become familiar with all the avenues available to market yourself. I spent many hours reading books, articles and reviewing websites and social media platforms.

To help assist you in building a personal career brand profile there are many online sources that are available in establishing media brand profiles.

Personal Career Brand marketing sources include:

Social media & networking
Social media has become a powerful career networking arena. There are many social media avenues and they are constantly changing and being added to. It is your responsibility to research and be active in those media.

Networking is a valuable tool and can be extremely useful in all areas of career change career branding. Networking demands considerable time and effort. In my case, I was limited in my initial networking of past associates, as I was venturing into new industries and businesses.

LinkedIn
LinkedIn is a premier career networking platform. It allows you to engage and participate with other users on a regular and consistent basis. It is one of the most effective business professional profile social media sites. LinkedIn is a business-oriented networking platform that involves millions of business professionals from around the world, representing hundreds of industries from more than 200 countries.

Your LinkedIn profile account is your own personal career brand. Considerable time and effort is required to create and present the account profile segments LinkedIn requires. Once your profile is completed, it is then possible to engage a vast network of professionals and build a network that will benefit you.

Personal business website
A career based professionally presented website is one of the most effective ways to build and promote your career brand.

The website requires extensive personal information and quality content that is appealing, engaging and informative. In addition to effective SEO (search engine optimization) implementation the website content should include all your key career information, including your brand profile; resume and career achievements; articles; awards; photos; videos; infographics and blogs. Your career profile and the content will attract positive attention from the online business community.

Blog
A business career orientated blog can be a significant plus. Creating an engaging and informative blog on your website on a consistent basis has proven to be a highly effective method of presenting your business talents to the online community. The blog should be focused on highlighting your business experience and knowledge. It should contain engaging and informative content that will attract business people. Creating a blog following will enhance your profile in the community.

I found creating and writing blogs to be of great benefit. It helped me to become known in the online community as an expert in my field of media. However, it took me a great deal of time and research to fully understand the art and craft of blogging and content creation.

Twitter
Twitter is an online networking platform that has become very prominent. It should be researched and utilized as an additional career building resource. Tweeting engaging and interesting career information will benefit your exposure and help build a following that often can generate career opportunities.

Other sources that can enhance your career visibility include:
Being active in professional, volunteer and civic associations, including colleges and universities. Public speaking at industry events especially in your field can be very beneficial.

Writing business articles, writing a business book and engaging in online discussions in your career field will only benefit your profile and demonstrate your expertise.

The internet and social media have become major resources for career change and career building. For the baby boomer, becoming familiar and practiced with these new avenues is a very important requirement.

> "What you get by achieving your goals is not as important as what you become by achieving your goals"
> **Henry David Thoreau**

CAREER OPPORTUNISM
What do I mean by career opportunism? Career opportunism refers to discovering and pursuing avenues that could potentially benefit your career path.

Being active and maintaining business connections, relationships and resources that may provide a business opportunity is an important part of career development. Pay attention to what is happening in the employment world and observing developments and changes in various sectors of industry.

Most importantly, should an opportunity arise, be in a position to access and act on the potential opening.

Let me illustrate career opportunism from my own experience.

I'm in my twenties working at a great job at 20th Century Fox. How could my world be more exciting and fulfilling? Then something out of the blue lands right on my lap!!!

I receive a call from an employment headhunter. He informs me about a job. This job involves the following:

- ✓ Promotion and pay increase
- ✓ Involves TV
- ✓ Worldwide event
- ✓ Huge recognition factor
- ✓ Involves sport
- ✓ Based in Los Angeles

How can this job exist? This job encompasses all the areas I love - namely, TV; sports; major event; in LA; huge exposure; sponsorship; significant responsibility; major promotion; world-wide project event; huge challenge and, oh yes, guaranteed termination within thirty months!

After being with 20th Century Fox for four years, this job opportunity drops on my desk – LUCK? Right place, right time?

One of the reasons I included this segment is that events can happen that may provide a major opportunity. In my case, the Summer Olympic Games were being held in Los Angeles within two years.

They needed management talent to organize putting on the Games. A golden opportunity dropped in my lap. (*career #3*)

Once the Olympics experience was completed the next major event that changed my career happened soon after, in the mid-nineteen eighties. The VHS video boom was just beginning. This was a huge technology event around the world that allowed every home access to play movies on their TV screens, via a VHS cassette player. The new VHS video cassette created an industry for producing and selling independent films to millions of people around the world to be played on home video cassette players.

Prior to the invention of the home video (VHS) and video cassette players, there was no industry. It was a technological revolution that created an industry and a worldwide business.

My talents, skills and interest in the entertainment industry allowed me to immediately identify with the new booming industry. I took advantage of the opportunity and the video industry took me on a fabulous journey of success and happiness beyond any of my dreams.

I created a new career for myself, as a self-employed film producer and distributor of film product around the world (*career #5*). I identified a huge opportunity in an infant industry that had huge potential. I was well-educated, European and well-travelled in the world. I quickly saw an opportunity to sell worldwide the movie VHS tapes.

I created a sales company to assist US producers sell their films around the world. For that service I took a percentage of the sales made. Soon, I had my own sales agency company and I was acquiring lots of films for sale around the world. I took a fee for every dollar of sales I made.

I loved that business model. Someone makes a product. You take that product and sell it to people around the world and take a fee. As long as demand was there you couldn't lose. Demand was there in a major way. It was like selling ice cream on a very hot day. For nearly ten years everyday was a hot day!

Everyone around the world wanted films on video.

The business model was very strong and lucrative:

- ✓ *Low risk – I acquired product already made*
- ✓ *Demand for product was huge*
- ✓ *Limited investment in marketing, etc. which I recouped from first sales*
- ✓ *I always got paid first from sales*
- ✓ *I was self-employed*
- ✓ *My business demanded lots of international travel*
- ✓ *I began making my own product for the booming market*
- ✓ *I was involved and responsible for all aspects of the video business; acquisition; distribution marketing; selling; delivery; collection; production; contracts; negotiations*

I greatly benefited from a technological event by starting my own company that provided me with so much, in so many ways, over many years.

Technological changes are happening and they create opportunities. Look at advances in digital technology, the internet and the explosion of social media. Find these new avenues and exploit them. The need to constantly be aware of changes and evaluating opportunities is of major importance to anyone wishing to change careers.

Examine some of the technological phases that have spawned significant events and major business changes over recent years:

- ✓ The PC phase
- ✓ The internet phase
- ✓ The web browsing phase
- ✓ The Social media explosion
- ✓ Smartphones; tablets

These events create opportunities for new careers and expanding old careers.

"The surest way to miss success is to miss the opportunity"
Victor Chasles

THINK

Thinking is really beneficial! Sounds silly... Think!

So many times, I have tried to apply my brain to figure out ways I could advance my career activities. I am constantly trying to come up with ideas, strategies to make things happen; ideas to deal with getting round roadblocks - trying to think outside of the box. Take time to allow your mind to mull over issues.

There are countless times during my career development, a seemingly insurmountable problem was overcome by a walk in the forest and letting my brain wander through different scenarios. Once an idea became viable then off I would go into action to see if it worked.

Think outside of the box... It really works!

"Forget all the reasons it won't work and believe the one reason that it will."

MAKE YOUR OWN LUCK

How important is luck in enhancing your career?

In my opinion very important! I am an example of how luck greatly contributed to my career.

The definition of luck can be stated as, a force that seems to operate for good or ill in a person's life, as in shaping circumstances or opportunities which are beyond our control. Is that really so? We often consider some people just lucky and others constantly unlucky.

Luck and the ability to generate luck may come from how a person performs or perceives themselves.

Research indicates that lucky people generate good fortune by ensuring positive behavior patterns, and therefore, positive outcomes occur. This includes creating and acting on chance opportunities; listening to their own intuition; creating positive expectations and having a positive attitude that creates a "lucky" environment. Being positive and having persistent optimism is truly beneficial. Making things happen is part of the process. Positive things will not happen if you do not act or are afraid to make decisions.

Find opportunities
Focus on your ability to identify new opportunities and take action when you find them. Be prepared to take risks and venture outside your comfort zone. Expand your horizons. Tap into the many avenues available on the internet. This includes but not limited to, online help communities like Meetup or LinkedIn where you can network and get advice.

Make it happen!
Should an opportunity become available, act quickly to evaluate and decide if it is worth pursuing? If it is, then act, do not procrastinate.

People who are thought of as "lucky" are skilled at creating, evaluating and acting upon chance opportunities.

I have spent some considerable time thinking about how lucky I have been in my life. Many people have commented on what a great career I have had and how lucky I have been.

But is it really LUCK?

- ✓ ***Was it luck….*** *I walked in to 20th Century Fox studios on that day; at that very time they were looking to fill certain positions, where my background and credentials fit their requirements?*

- ✓ ***Was it luck….*** *I was offered a position at the Olympic Games Organizing Committee? The Olympic Games which are held every four years and this was in LA?*

- ✓ ***Was it luck….*** *On my return to England after being in LA and at the Olympic Games, my old financial consulting firm was expanding their involvement with entertainment clients especially film and I popped up with all my experience and was offered a job?*

- ✓ ***Was it luck….*** *On my way back to the USA after my year in England, I was introduced to the owner of one of the largest and most progressive video companies in Germany, who had a good friend in Zurich Switzerland, who was looking to partner up with*

> someone in a new film company in Los Angeles, funded by a South African investor?
>
> ✓ **Was it luck....** I started my own company at the beginning of a new media technology in the film world, namely home video, and I was based in Los Angeles, the epic center of this new film revenue stream?
>
> ✓ **Was it luck....** At the University of Miami, I walked in to the Business School just as they were looking for a new faculty member for Marketing?
>
> ✓ **Was it luck....** At the University of Miami, the School of Communication, Motion Picture dept. needed a replacement lecturer on film marketing, just as I arrived?
>
> Was it luck, fate or just coincidence?
>
> I firmly believe that you can make your own luck. However, you have to go find those opportunities. Research, investigate, call, inquire and be totally one hundred percent proactive in your career activities - then luck will find you!

"What are the odds that the next person you meet will change your day, your career?"

Proactive and determined

Be proactive, hardworking and determined. These qualities will ultimately pay dividends for you, both in the present and in the future. Having these qualities will definitely improve your luck and create a positive atmosphere. If you don't believe in yourself and your skills, no one else will! If at first you do not succeed, try again! Rarely is career development a sprint, more a marathon.

HANDLE STRESS

Stress happens!

We generally use the word "stress" when we feel that everything seems to have become too much. When we are stressed we feel overloaded and wonder whether we really can cope.

Limited stress can motivate and help performance. However, when stress is applied constantly your mind and body pay the price. Beyond a certain point, stress stops being helpful and starts causing major damage to your health, your productivity, your relationships and your quality of life.

It's important to learn how to recognize when your stress levels are getting excessive. Everyone handles stress differently. Possible action may include reducing your work load, more exercise, talking with friends, or even seeking professional help. Ignoring stress can and often is counter-productive and can lead to serious problems.

During the Olympic Games (career #3), we had definitive deadlines that could not be altered, namely the Olympic Games began on a set date, with billions of people watching the TV for the Olympic Games Opening Ceremonies.

We had thousands of deadlines and we literally worked 24 hours a day. The Games had stress on stress. I learnt many lessons from being part of the LAOOC (Los Angeles Olympic Organizing Committee).

I realized that I could take a great deal of stress, but many of my co-workers could not. Pushing and pushing people to perform, can cause severe problems. Some staff members needed positive reinforcement and praise while others responded to a more harsh tone. As a manager, it was part of our responsibility to customize responses for each individual, in order to help them be the most effective.

Many people were let go because they could not keep up with the work load and the constant pressure to perform and perform well. Deadlines could not be missed.

"If you're going through hell, keep going."
Rodney Atkins

LEARN FROM MISTAKES
It's a fact – we make mistakes and we have failures!

It's how we handle those mistakes and failures that determines the future outcome. Learning to use failure to our benefit is one of the most important lessons we can ever learn.

It's human nature to focus on failures instead of success. Success validates our strengths, skills, abilities and provides confidence in future ventures. Failures tend to undermine our confidence and self-esteem.

Our ability to place failure and mistakes in the correct context is important. When dealing with failure and mistakes, focus on understanding why the mistakes happened. Making mistakes is part of business and part of life. Learn from failures.

Many successful people have suffered major failures in their journey through life. Failure is not the end of the world - it is merely a bump on the road to success. A failure should be evaluated, lessons learned and then applied to your next venture.

Do not allow fear of failure to deter you from making bold decisions. By not acting we might persuade ourselves that we minimize our chances of failure; however, by ensuring you research and evaluate potential decisions thoroughly and weigh up the pros and cons with care, then a decision is based on information and skill. That decision can be made from confidence. If it does not work then go back and reassess. We should not be hindered by fear or inaction.

Like most people who have been in business for many years, I have had my fair share of failures.

One of my biggest failures was not anticipating a major shift in demand for a film project I was producing. This was one of my recent business ventures. Please go for more detail to the chapter MY CAREER AFTER FIFTY.

Failure can come in all forms and sizes. It may be a failure of a sales target or a failure in a business relationship – keep failure in proportion and never let it overwhelm you.

Turn failure into a positive and create a learning experience you can apply next time for your benefit. Failures should not depress you or affect your drive to succeed.

Try and try and try again, but learn from your mistakes.

> *"Make failure your teacher, not your undertaker."*
> Zig Zigla

WORK TO LIVE OR LIVE TO WORK

Such an interesting question! I personally think that we should work to live and not the latter. Why focus on living to work? Seems life has so much more to offer than just working! Balance is required between work, family and your social life. It is your decision to create the balance that best suits you.

In Europe, vacation is a priority to most people. In a recent research poll of many western countries, using many variables and parameters, the "happiest" country was Denmark. USA was way down the list.

Not surprisingly, the study clearly stated that having enough leisure time affects a person's mental health and strongly impacts happiness. In the higher ranking countries, leisure time and vacation were major factors and were listed as a high priority.

Should we look at the quality of life rather than quantity in our life? Money and materiality are not everything!

Do we really think money can buy happiness? The attitude of work more, get more money so we will be happier… Is that really true?

Our work can and often does lead to more stress and potentially a lower quality of life. There are few things that stress us out on a consistent basis more than our work, especially when it takes away from all of the other things that life has to offer. Stress is the number one cause of health problems (mental and physical).

Research has highlighted some interesting bits of information:

- ✓ The U.S. remains the only industrialized country in the world that has no legally mandated annual vacation.
- ✓ In most western countries there are approximately twenty to thirty-five paid vacation days per year. In the USA paid vacation is optional for employers.
- ✓ Only about fifty percent of US workers take the full allocation of vacation time.
- ✓ Americans work one hundred and thirty-seven more hours per year than Japanese workers; two hundred and fifty more hours per year more than English workers and nearly five hundred more hours per year than French workers. Even so, research indicates US workers have similar productivity per year.

So do you live to work or work to live?

In my humble opinion, America has got vacations all wrong and Europe has it right.

We should have at least one month off with pay and we should all take that time off. That's my opinion.

Let's work to live, not live to work.

Work is fine and is a necessity on many fronts, but to have quality time for yourself, family and friends for a reasonable amount of time just seems civilized. To have so little vacation time in a full year of hard work is criminal!

Being from Europe, I see the benefits vacations have for the spirit and the body. Having time away to re-charge your batteries is a must. I see the US system and I have lived the European system. Regarding vacations, Europe wins.

**"The greatest mistake you can make in life
is to be continually fearing you will make one."
Elbert Hubbard**

SUMMARY

A blueprint has been provided to you. It is there to assist you in completing a major goal in your life... Changing Careers!

**FIVE STEP APPROACH TO CAREER CHANGE SUCCESS
FOR BABY BOOMERS**

- **WHAT DO YOU WANT**
- **WHERE ARE YOU NOW**
- **WHAT YOU NEED TO HAVE**
- **HOW TO GET THERE**
- **WHAT YOU NEED TO DO**

In each chapter, there is a wealth of information to help you through the overwhelming task of changing careers.

I hope, I have presented the material in an organized and proficient manner that is both inspiring and motivational.

The final object being that you do indeed, find a career that provides you the level of fulfillment, happiness and satisfaction you wish for.

The task of career change is not an easy one. It demands a great deal of work, motivation, dedication and exceptional perseverance to stay the course and attain your goals.

I hope my personal experiences, highlighted continuously in the book, provide you inspiration and motivation to accomplish your goal.

**A successful career change will change your life for the better.
It did for me! Good luck on your journey!**

I CHOOSE...

TO LIVE BY CHOICE, NOT BY CHANCE;
TO MAKE CHANGES, NOT EXCUSES;
TO BE MOTIVATED, NOT MANIPULATED;
TO BE USEFUL, NOT USED;
TO EXCEL, NOT COMPETE;
I CHOOSE SELF-ESTEEM, NOT SELF-PITY;
I CHOOSE TO LISTEN TO MY INNER VOICE,
NOT THE RANDOM OPINION OF OTHERS.

-Skarleth HDZ

KEEP YOUR THOUGHTS POSITIVE
BECAUSE YOUR THOUGHTS BECOME
YOUR WORDS

KEEP YOUR WORDS POSITIVE
BECAUSE YOUR WORDS BECOME
YOUR BEHAVIOR

KEEP YOUR BEHAVIOR POSITIVE
BECAUSE YOUR BEHAVIOR BECOME
YOUR HABITS

KEEP YOUR HABITS POSITIVE
BECAUSE YOUR HABITS BECOME
YOUR VALUES

KEEP YOUR VALUES POSITIVE
BECAUSE YOUR VALUES BECOME
YOUR DESTINY

- Mahatma Gandhi

JOHN RODSETT – AUTHOR

John is an award winning book author, charismatic speaker, business owner, international entrepreneur, seminar presenter, university lecturer and **Baby Boomer!**

His book "Change Your Career... Baby Boomers" (a motivational career guide) has been widely acclaimed as a significant contribution in providing people who wish to change careers, a detailed template for career change, tailored to their specific circumstances, skills and experience.

This dynamic and motivating career speaker presents a clear, direct and practical approach to "changing your career" with focused and highly effective winning strategies. With John's charismatic presentation and English humor, he provides innovative tools and techniques that will inspire and provide a career roadmap to ensure you are the right path to career change success.

John has had an exceptional career as a university lecturer at two of the top universities in America, (University of Miami & University of Washington) where his expertise was Marketing and Global Business. His teaching and speaking style are innovative, highly motivational and effective.

He is a recognized authority in media and entertainment business sectors, having extensive business experience with major companies such as 20th Century Fox and the Summer Olympic Games organization. His exceptional entrepreneurial business ventures include owning an international media distribution company, world-wide marketing/sales and business consulting in a variety of business sectors.

John has five books published about the independent film business and is acknowledged as an expert in that field.

JOHN RODSETT - <u>BIO-ACHIEVEMENTS–EDUCATION</u>

TOUCHE ROSS
(Big Eight Accounting Firm, Audit Senior- Four yrs.)

London, England
- Chrysler
- General Electric
- Rolls Royce

20TH CENTURY FOX
(TV Executive/ Film - Four years)

Los Angeles, CA
- "Alien"
- "MASH TV series"
- TV Division

SUMMER OLYMPIC GAMES
(Vice President, Controller- Three years)

Los Angeles Olympic ames- 1984
- Start-up & closed out - $1b. event
- Profit - $250 M

CHIEF MEDIA CONSULTANT
(One of the World's Largest Accounting/Financial Consulting Firms- One year)

London, England
- Duran Duran
- Working Title
- Wimbledon Tennis

FILM PRODUCTION & DISTRIBUTION COMPANY
(Owner - LA & Zurich- Twenty years)
(www.mrfilmbiz.com)

Los Angeles/Zurich
- Produced twenty-one independent films
- Sales Agent- distributed & consulted worldwide on over two hundred films

UNIVERSITY PROFESSSOR
(Full time/part time Adjunct Professor – Five years:
- *School of Business*
- *School of Communication)*

Miami & Seattle
- University of Miami
- University of Washington

BOOK AUTHOR
(Numerous titles published to present)

Books Published:
- "The Film Biz Bible" - 2011
- "501 Things You Need to Know" - 2013
- "Change Your Career Change Your Life" - Motivational Career Guide

SPEAKER & SEMINARS
(To Present)

Speaker/Seminar Topics:
- Film Business/Events
- Career Motivation/ Career Change
- *www.mrfilmbiz.com*
- *www.johnrodsett.com*

EDUCATION:

Degrees & Professional Education
- **University of Nottingham (England)** Industrial Economics Honors BA Degree
- **Old Dominion University (USA)** Masters of Science Degree
- **Professional Education** Chartered Accountancy (UK) Touche Ross Four yrs. Finance/ Accounting MBA equivalent

BUSINESS – GENERAL:
- 20TH Century Fox Studios – Manager/Controller * Fox Sports * MASH TV Series
- Los Angeles Olympic Games Organizing Committee – VP Controller
- Touche Ross – Audit Senior * Rolls Royce * General Electric * Chrysler Cars
- Touche Ross – Media Consultant * Music and Entertainment clients
- Feature Film & Documentary Producer
- International Distributor – Media * Film * Marvel Comics CD games * Documentaries
- University Professor (Full Time, Adjunct) *University of Miami, School of Business
- University Professor (Adjunct) * University of Washington, Business Program
- Book Author
- Seminar & Motivational Speaker
- Business Consultant

BOOK AUTHOR:
- Book Title: "Change Your Career… Baby Boomers" – 2014
- Book Title: "The Film Biz Bible" – 2013
- Book Title: "501 Things You Should Know About The Indie Film Business"
- Book Title: "Marketing, Distribution, Selling – The Film Biz" - 2013
- Book Title: "Producing, Creative – The Film Biz" -2013
- Book Title: "Film Financing – The Film Biz" – 2013
- Numerous articles for business and media journals

MEDIA BUSINESS:
- 20th Century Fox – MASH TV Series * Fox Sports * Various TV series
- 1984 Summer Olympic Games – Worldwide TV * Coca Cola * Xerox * NBC Network
- Film Producer – Twenty one Executive Producer & Producer credits
- Media Projects included * Marvel / X Men * Lucille Ball * OJ Simpson *Paul Watson/Green Peace * Pope John Paul II

UNIVERSITY LECTURER:
- University Professor (Adjunct) *University of Miami, School of Business - Marketing - Full Time 2005 to 2007
- University Professor (Adjunct) * University of Washington, Business Program - Marketing & Global Business – 2008 to 2010

OTHER BOOKS BY JOHN RODSETT

- "The Film Biz Bible"
- "501 Things You Should Know About The Indie Film Business"
- "Marketing, Distribution, Selling - The Film Biz Bible"
- "Producing, Creative - The Film Biz Bible"
- "Film Financing - The Film Biz Bible"

Available on www.amazon.com

ACKNOWLEDGEMENTS

Ever since I left England and moved to the USA some 30 years ago, I have been very aware of my career and the steps I have taken to maximize my potential. Over these many years and especially over the last ten years, I have accumulated vast amounts of data, articles, books, internet information on the topic of careers from hundreds of sources. I have talked to many very smart and knowledgeable people and read hundreds of articles, case studies, books, internet blogs, internet articles and trade papers - far too many to mention. My own experiences and day to day business involvement over these many years has also provided me a huge reservoir of knowledge. The combination of all these sources has contributed to this book. I cannot in truth, list all of these sources but please know I acknowledge everyone that has contributed to my experience in understanding life, career and career changes.

www.ingramcontent.com/pod-product-compliance
Lightning Source LLC
Chambersburg PA
CBHW051710170526
45167CB00002B/616